SYMPHONY OF DESIRE

Myth in the Mainstream Indian English Novel

SYMPHONY OF DESIRE

Myth in the Mainstream Indian English Novel

Nalini Shyam Kamil

ADHYAYAN

ADHYAYAN PUBLISHERS & DISTRIBUTORS

NEW DELHI (INDIA)

Published by
ADHYAYAN PUBLISHERS & DISTRIBUTORS
4378/4B, 105, J.M.D. House, Murari Lal Street
Ansari Road Darya Ganj, New Delhi - 110002
Ph.: 011-23263018, 011-23277156, Fax: 011-23280028
Email: adhyayanpublishers@yahoo.com

Symphony of Desire: Myth in the Mainstream Indian English Novel

Edition 2010
ISBN 978-81-8435-217-7

Printed in India

Published by Harish Chandra Yadav for Adhyayan Publishers & Distributors, Delhi. Laser Typesetting at A. V. Rao and Printed at Tarun Offset Printers, Delhi

Dedicated to

Late Pt. Ram Karan Shukla,

my great grand father-

who brought me up and made me what I am.

Foreword

When ether, air, fire and water conjoin the infinite radiance of the soul, a being is constituted out of necessities and compulsions that take the form of a universal Destiny which, is in theistic terms, God's will to multiply and become many from being one. The rudimentary elements are the first born of Nature-Nature being God's creative energy also known as *Maya* in the *Bhagavadgita* and *Vedanta*. The union of the earth and the sky is the first cause for the coming into existence of procreated beings. Myths are forms of appropriation of the super-mundane reality that is neither explainable nor understandable. It is for this reason that the *Purush-Sukta* of the *Rig Veda* describes three-fourth of the *Purusha* only because that much is visible. The rest is left for imagination to surmount and replenish. Imagination, therefore, is the aetiological factor behind the production of all kinds of myths, religions, secular, among the rest.

Imagination is given to man by God so that man could search for his origins. Origins do not have a beginning nor an end for such concepts are germinated by a temporality which itself is dependent upon eternity which has no pre-fabricated structures of either the mind or the body. Time and space do not serve as *priori* conditions for its existence. Imagination is the eternal body of things as William Blake said wherein our naked lineaments in varied forms, colours and textures lie. Imagination is another space; it is the transcendental expropriation of God. Imagination, therefore, is inside as well as outside time. To that extent, it has the power to fragment all organisms and constitute them again. The binaries are sublunary devices within Imagination that become manifest in the world of time. Time is a negative utopia, an inverted bell, a cacophony carrying the load of divergently organized jarring sounds. The transcendental is transcendental to the extent we are able to imagine it as such. All human angles to transcendentalism are still a form of time, and to that extent, they continue to create mystery what would otherwise be revelation.

Mythologies are pragmatic acts of consciousness on the part of man aimed at understanding his existence in relation to objects of Nature he finds himself surrounded by. Language is the result of a compulsion characterized by the inner burdens man carries with himself. Language is the first born of time-opulence yet poverty, an expressive mode yet a banal exercise. Misfortunes befell man because he could not understand himself without language. Language, as a result, cried in pain and anguish because it could provide no more. Man felt incapacitated and drained out. When the language could not do it, the hieroglyph emerged on the surface of desire. The hieroglyph had a larger abundance of foregrounding and appropriation; it provided man with a shelter he could not have found any where. God became an image and the image transcended itself by itself. There fore the mystery again that produced the myth. Going beyond History into imagination, hieroglyphs were the first to emerge on the temporal scene as they bridged, or so it seemed, the gap between eternity and time, the unmanifest and the manifest, the unknown and the known.

God loaded Imagination with all kinds of potentialities which had the power to germinate, given the proper soil, moisture and the environment. The distinction between the sacred and the profane is as old as the creation itself or so new as we may call it. As the Ages from the Golden to the Iron descend, the consciousness becomes more and more constricted, confiscated so to say, and disappears in the materiality of existence that is the bane of civilization. In the Golden Age, there is no Freudian 'unconscious' with its instinctual drives and desires for sexual hegemony resulting in patriarchical and matriarchal structures. This age has a free play of imagination which juxtaposes nothing with nothing because perfection is the goal of human existence. Perfection is not the material possession of objects but the realization being as existing within God. Such appropriations had a full range of possibilities that were realized to the maximum because the time growth was such and man's mental fabrications had not been corrupted. The unconscious had the quest theme and the origin was the target. Origins, though, are all forms of mediations for beginnings and ends are not known as Krishna says in the *Bhagavadgita*. Only the middles are known and they constitute a fragmented temporality that cannot give us even the sense of the origin. Using a temporal language to account for the secrets of imagination will not get us any where. Man, though, has been trying to accomplish the same only across the ages. The unconscious, therefore, in the Golden Age, is a portion of God that has yet not malleated itself into any thing different. It cries for the land of Nativity and gets in good measure.

As we slide down further into the temporality's junctural points, the locus of the unconscious shifts from being towards God for now it gradually has looked for another habitation and a name where a consciousness of the body is ever ready to do the damage. The hieroglyph is getting rounded off, and, over a period of time, it loses its own nomenclatures of identity. The Bronze Age sees misrepresentation of the identity process which is well on its way to self-distortion. Eternity weeps but the claims of the body become larger than those of the soul. The Iron Age has come. Man has become a villain committing theft in his own house, claiming victorious where defeats are unaccountable. The stage of human life could not have been worse than this. The language that succeeded the hieroglyph found a double within itself for the villain hid himself within it and would not allow the truth to emerge. This resulted in the production of the myths of the profane that diluted and ultimately destroyed what, otherwise, was an eternal portion of God Himself.

Cultures are born as mythemes; They are unaccounted programmes of conceptions waiting to breed reality afresh and a myriad times. The *Vedic* culture is based upon *yajnas,* sacrificial retuals. They consolidate themselves upon the recurring theme that God-begotten must be returned to God and rituals of sacrifice can alone do it. So, all the seed elements join fire that offers oblations to God who then blesses man and creation with fertility of all kinds. *Vedas* celebrate powers of Nature but this is an under statement because they celebrate a power that is beyond the powers of Nature. That is the secret of Indian epistemological tradition. *Dvani* or suggestion, is a mode of Imagination with the help of which God can be appropriated. For literary Studies, therefore, texts are God's formal lineaments; authorial intentions are God's tenalitien, and the finished texts is still Searching for God because that search is the only search the writer as a *sadhaka* can undertake. The four *Vedas* are the four sides of the narrative which is in its seed form in the *chhandas* which are the bodies of gods and goddesses. The narrative of the Bunyan tree, as a result, is immanent in the bunyan seed which is tiny beyond imagination. The Indian narrative tradition is like a spider's web having the infinite capacities of weaving the warp and the woof of the world. The ritualistic galore in the *Yajur* and *Atharva vedas* suggests the infinite sense of man towards the carnivalesque-the breeding of metaphors- all from the body that duplicate, triplicate, quadruplicate, the given segments of reality myriad times and in myriad ways.

Upanishads are the phenomenologies of the human spirit. When the *Vedic* rituals churned objects in order to make an exposition, the expositions acquired a nomadic structure so to say; *Aranyakas* were the play-fields of the *Vedic* folk-lore and it decimated into the seed syllables when rooted to meditational postures and creative ontologies. *Upanishads,* thus, became thought processes' extreme galore, an ideational climax that as much prohibited narrative groundings as it expounded them in its own way. It was the *bija-rupa* reductionism of the thought process that finally fore grounded the birth of the narrative in its widest and deepest of scriptural gestures. *Puranas* elucidated the Body of God as the disjunctural play of *Maya* the illusory power that makes tangible relationships at will and breaks them as well. Narratives are forms of *Maya* for they generate the semblance of reality which does not become a process of achieving identity.

All narrativization begs the question: 'where to from here'? Indian art of narratology, therefore, places some form or the other of God at the centre while the discursive details acquire a cyclic pattern. Of the eighteen recognized *Puranas,* Krishna/Vishnu cycles are the post predominant feature to emerge. The movement has its rotundity and the rotundity has its illusions. Illusions, though, cross refer to God-the supreme episteme and the giver of all nomenclatures. The still point of a moving world is God Himself who disseminates thereby producing aesthetic principles for the enjoyment of the created universe. Genealogies foreground narrative patterns in the *Puranas*. There is, therefore, a meta-narrative always taking shape as gods and goddesses evolve into functional and endless substitutionry powers that designate the core argument of the narrative. *Bhagavad Purana*, thus, is the Body of Krishna just as *Puranas* assigned to Vishnu and Shiva are the body textures of those gods. History in the *Puranas* acquires a mythopoeic character. Indian narratology does not believe in the linearity of progression which is banal; it dos not believe in the empirical recording of details either. It generates belief patterns on the contrary whose aim is not really the knowledge of what did happen but what has been revealed and realized. This distinguishes Indian narratology from its western counterpart where loveless details follow one after another and the reader becoming no worthier than before as by the end of the day he is just in the possession of a few details with the help of which he can draw the empirical outlines of a particular object. History has no being but a concatenated intertwining that ultimately falls upon itself and dies.

This is the exodus of meaning, the same as Meses getting into the wilderness and ever trying to get to the promised land but never quite.

Ramcharit Manas and *Mahabharata* are the two grand epics in the Indian tradition in the apocalyptic mode. The former takes a linear route to progressevity's utter climaxes, the latter unfolds truths of life in episodic structures to which consciousness is tied down. Lord Ram stands at the centre of *Ramcharit Manas*, the still point that mediates temporal flux in proportions not easily imaginable. Krishna, on the contrary, is the transcendental episteme of the *Mahabharata*, a human figure yet a god, a Hero without acts yet standing behind all acts ever performed. Ram's patience is not only enveloping but tantalizing too; it seems to puncture the narrative upon which it builds its own figural lineaments. Ram-Ravan narative is mediated by Lord Hanuman who then becomes the progenitor of causality as well as the begetter of effects. The sequential progression of *Ramcharit Manas* respects both the chronology as well as the genealogy of the Hero involved. As a result, Ram has a pretty definable character as opposed to Krishna whose beginnings and ends are not known. Krishna has an unpredictability about Himself; He is willingly violating linearity, progression, sequencing, in order to constitute a figure which is never constitutable. Ram is classical while Krishna is Romantic in the highest traditions in the history of the meaning of those terms. Ram preserves a system,- Krishna breaks a system in order to break fresh grounds. Krishna is a deconstructor *par excellence*. The instincts and the motivational components of human personality are at their worst and best in the *Mahabharata.*

The *Bible* as the supreme Text of the Western canon has an episodic structure too. The Pentateuch though seems to be a grounding of a different Kind. The old and the New Testaments are the classic and the romantic possibilities of the Western canon. Blake said that Moses acted by rules while Jesus acted by inspiration and imagination. The ontological status of the two testaments is clear enough. Jesus, St. Augustine, Ezekiel are prophets of a new breed for they do not shy away from influences originating from the East. Ezekiel's vision, therefore, is similar to that of Krishna's cosmic form where the outside becomes the inside and *vice versa.* Narrative traditions, thus, are grounded in cultural specifities, a localized folk-lore religion, which grows and evolves into the official corner stones of an established religion that we call Hinduism or christianty. Western narrative though, becomes a victim of nature/ culture dichotomy, thus resulting in ruptures and aporias. Indian narrative, on the other hand, has a cognitive integrity which warrants tremendous powers of assimilation and reproduction. There is no dichotomy of any kind here leave alone nature/culture for every minute detail created is part of God, hence a revelation unto itself. The text is born at each sensory empire that the mind can lay claim to. The mind supplies the binaries, trinaries while the **buddhi** or the soul synchronises them into a unity bringing them inclose proximity to the **Atman** which then be gets eternity on the palm of one's hand as Blake said.

Indian English literature originates from the sources that forestall *Rig Veda* and the rest of the literary-cultural ambience. *Panchtantra, Katha Sarit Sager, Bhagavat Puran*, among others, form the core of Indian art of narratology. Allegory is the governing mode and motif for it facilitates an endless expansion of the minutest of details in terms of space realities. The symbol is the temporal journey of the narrative while archetype its recurring pattern. Myth is the body which distributes essence at various allegorical levels. The narrative occupies a quest theme, the quest often resulting in revelation and salvation which falls consequent upon it. Layerings, therefore, are discursive networkings, the textual folies that have the capacity to grow and multiply. The realm of interiorisation is infinite. It has to be as it is because the beginnings and the ends are not known. What is known is the middle. This middle becomes the gyrating axis, the **spiritus mundi**, of the whole world. All this leads to the experience that the nothing begets nothing and that is the way to perfection and completeness. Only three-fourth of the **Purusha** is narratable, the rest is lost to the eyesight and is substituted by imagination only in a script-less realm.

Raja Rao's novels aim to accomplish precisely this. He organizes a scheme of characters, situations, discussions and dialogue in a way and in a manner that the quest theme occupies the core. The function of the narrative becomes the production of the discriminative intellect which finally helps the mind leave the body in favour of the soul which is a portion of God Himself. Raja Rao, therefore, is looking for revelation in prose rhythms that shape the contours of our being, uplift it, finally sustaining it in the supreme principles of identity. Mulk Raj Anand, R.K. Narayan have Buddhist and Marxist apertures embalmed to their thought Processes. They write for the marginalized, the disgraced and the down trodden so that the narrative cleanses itself of the dross it has acquired over the ages. Sulman Rushdie assimilates, like the **Puranas**, an incredible amount of History, myth, legend and folk-tale, envisioning a polysemy that is so characteristic of the Indian tradition. Shashi Tharoor and the rest of the Postmodernist Indian English novelists including Arundhti Roy, make consciousness itself the Hero which is seeking meaning out of aperias spread all round. Sulman Rushdie, with all his romance with language, history, myth, amalgamating consciousness, remains a novelist in the secular tradition as for him this world is too important to be transcended or glossed over and then left alone. Raja Rao's use of myth is redemptive while Anand and Narayan use myths for social integration and for generating efficacious social structure which can contribute to the meaningful growth of the country.

Nalini Shyam Kamil has ventured into a complex field with multiple epistemes warring at each other in consonance or deformity producing, in the process, high and low-mimetic structures of experience and consciousness. Nalini maintains a simple line of argument defining myth in its normative aspects, bringing out its cyclic and cultural character with the help of available scholarship. His analysis of the mainstream novels undertaken for study is satisfactory, even promising, for it is able to do justice to the textual compulsions warranted. Myths corroborate the history of a nation and Nalini shows it pretty well. *Symphony of Desire* more than envelops the encyclopaedic range of Indian reality which is so divergent, pluralistic, multi-ethnic and multi-cultural. To bind all these elements into a single folktale stage of high and low mimetic drama is a tribute not only to the Indian English writers but also to those who make studies of such traditions possible. Nalini has adopted a formalistic approach without pretensions. He remains intelligible, understandable and readable. For a beginner, one cannot ask for more.

Charu Sheel Singh

Professor

Department of English

Mahatma Gandhi Kashi Vidyapith

Varanasi

Preface

Myths trace back the history of consciousness from primordial times to the present in an endlessly ongoing process. That is how C.G. Jung and Michel Foucault have tried to understand mythical constructions available in the history of mankind. Malinouski finds myth as constituting a cyclic pattern beginning with the birth of a child, and passing through different ritual phases, attaining salvational ends which in the Indian tradition is the gateway to immortality. Myths, therefore, can have linear historical structures, temporal-cyclical structures, and historical transcendental structures which have spiral ends. Arnold Toynbee, Oswald Spenglar and Sir J.G. Frazer, evolved a cyclic view of mythical narratives which ground history in temporality. However, in the Indian tradition, mythological history is not only cyclic but also spiral which makes myths, histories and narratives immortal.

The present book entitled *Symphony of Desire* aims at critically examining the mainstream Indian English novel which is represented by Raja Rao's *The Serpent and the Rope*, R.K. Narayan's *The Man Eater of Malgudi*, Salman Rushdie's *Midnight's Children*, Amitav Ghosh's *The Circle of Reason* and Shashi Tharoor's *The Great Indian Novel*. There are some sporadic writings on the use of myth in these novels but no comprehensive work has yet been done on the use of myth in Indian Novels in English, especially on the novels written during post-Nehru era. The present book especially explores the structural constituents on the basis of mythic paradigms on these novels. The present study critically analyses the multiple uses of myth in the novels undertaken for the study.

The book is divided into seven chapters followed by a detailed bibliography. The *first* chapter focuses on the origin, meaning, functions of myth and its relationship with fiction. It also discusses the extensive use of myth in Indian English narrative tradition.

The *second* chapter undertakes to study Raja Rao's novel *The Serpent and the Rope* which comprises layers of religion, ritual, metaphysics, myth, legend and folklore. The novel is written on the *Puranic* pattern. It is episodic and digressional. Multiple stories are woven into the seminal theme of the novel that exhibit an urgency of time which lead to semantic pluralism.

The *third* chapter deals with R.K. Narayans's use of myth as metaphor in the novel *The Man Eater of Malgudi*. Metaphor fosters a double vision of life in reality and crystallized symbolism. The novelist uses it as a powerful weapon which facilitates his novels a simple and smooth reading.

The *fourth* chapter tries to analyse and evaluate Salman Rushdie's use of a variety of myths in *Midnight's Children*. Rushdie has used several Hindu and Greek myths in the novel. The novel employs a mythical framework of narrative of the historical and political situation and contextualizes it to Indian political scenario. This method of juxtaposing the present with the past leads to the unfolding of the layers of suggestivity levels which are numerous.

The *fifth* chapter discusses Amitav Ghosh's paradigmatic use of myth in the novel *The Circle of Reason*. It is a highly mythical novel as it associates the Nachiketa myth of the Upanishadic era with the present age of science and reason.

The *sixth* chapter structurally examines the mythic texture in *The Great Indian Novel*. The novel is written on the model of ancient epic the *Mahabharata*. Myth in the novel carries burdens of contemporary reality which it contextualizes and cross refers at various levels.

The *seventh* chapter is inclined to the view that myth is a shaping principle which informs the creative gestures of the text.

This book is an improved version of my Ph.D. thesis that I submitted to V. B. S. Purvanchal University, Jaunpur in the year 2007. In the accomplishment of this task I humbly acknowledge the guidance, support and continuous cooperation of Dr. B. L.

Misra, Dr. Lalji Misra, Prof. Charu Sheel Singh, Prof. M.K. Choudhury my family and all the teachers of the department of English, B.H.U, Varanasi. My thanks are also due to the library staff of Banaras Hindu University, Varanasi, Delhi University, Delhi and Jawaharlal Nehru University, New Delhi who ungrudgingly helped me to provide study materials as required by me from time to time. Lastly, I record my gratefulness to the critics and scholars whose views have been cited in this book.

—Nalini Shyam Kamil

Contents

Foreword vii

Preface xv

1. Myth: Texts and Contexts in Indian English Fiction 1
2. *The Serpent and the Rope*: Mythic Dimensions 26
3. *The Man Eater of Malgudi*: Myth as Metaphor 52
4. *Midnight's Children*: Mythic Labyrinth 76
5. *The Circle of Reason*: Mythic Paradigm 103
6. *The Great Indian Novel*: Mythic Texture 122
7. Conclusion 141

Bibliography 147

Index 156

I

Myth: Texts and Contexts in Indian English Fiction

The word 'myth' is derived from the Greek word 'Muthos', which originally meant a tale, and in a wider sense, a statement, a story or the plot of a play. For Plato, the first known user of the term, 'Muthologia', myth meant simply the telling of stories[1]. The word came into existence as a fabulous or fictitious tale. Gradually, the word acquired a more specific connotation and came to be identified with a story or narrative in which gods or supernatural agencies played the vital role. The opening part of the chapter shall undertake a study of the structural components of myth that constitute its essential narrative. This will be done with the help of available scholarship with a view to providing a perspective to the ideas developed in subsequent portions of the chapter.

Mark Schorer considered myth as "fundamental, the dramatic representation of our deepest instinctual life, of a primary awareness of man in the universe, capable of many configurations, upon which all particular opinions and attitudes depend."[2] Myth thus became a milestone of human civilization, creating codes of belief, faith in rituals and principles of morality. Myth choreographs nature and creatively disseminates the productive variance available to human consciousness. The traditional tale which is common to the members of a tribe, race,community or nation, generally involves the supernatural beings that denote some natural phenomenon. Professor V. Rai in his unpublished Ph.D. Dissertation titled *Use of Myth in the Poetry of the Romantic Revival*, thus, explains:

The roots of ancient myths are hidden in the depth of unrecorded time, hence no feet of historical imagination enables the reader to visualize explicitly the circumstances and conditions connected with their birth, growth, expansion, amalgamation and ramifications. The psychologists, anthropologists and the readers of primitive religions have succeeded to a very large extent in dissipating the obscurity and paving the way for a proper understanding of the nature and significance of the ancient myths.[3]

P. Lal, another Indian poet-critic, points out the immense cultural significance of myth:

> Myth holds communities and races more strongly than language, territory and government, myth provides insights into the mysteries of life and death with a poetic richness that has startling truth and immediacy. There is no secular substitute for truth.[4]

According to Mircea Eliade, myths are the systems which constitute the body of metaphysics. He observes:

> The metaphysical concepts of the archaic world were not always formulated in theoretical language, but the symbol, the myth and the rite express on different planes and through the means proper to them, a complex system of coherent affirmations about the ultimate reality of things, a system that can be regarded as constituting a metaphysics.[5]

Myth is thus a symbolic narrative of unknown origin which is partly traditional and professedly relates actual events with convictions that acquire a religious structure over a period of time. Elizabeth Drew finds the perspective in using myth in modern literature as a symbol equating and expressing the human experience:

> The mythical method is the representation of experience in symbolic form, the earliest and still the most direct and immediate form of human experience.[6]

Myth facilitates a possibility of structures which have contemporary connotations. In the words of Malionovski:

> Myth is to a native neither a fictitious study nor an account of a dead past; it is a statement of bigger reality still particularly alive. It is alive in its precedent, its law, and its moral, still rule

the social life of the natives. What really matters about such a story is its social function. It conveys the fundamental fact of the local unity of the group of people descendent from the common ancestor.[7]

Another feature of myth is the extremely cultural context, which narrates a sacred history and reveals the facts behind 'true history'. Myths relate supernatural interpretations for natural phenomena and deal with cosmic subjects like creation and death. Myths germinate in collective unconscious of the mankind assuming textures that become narrative patterns with an idiom that is a creative writer's own. Romilla Thapar rightly argues, "Myth at one level is a straight forward story, a narrative; at another it reflects the integrating values around which societies are organized."[8]

Myth associates the individual mind with universal phenomenon. Therefore, the study of mythology evokes the cultural heritage of people and society. The opinion of M.H. Abrams is relevant here to observe:

One story in a mythology ... a system of hereditary stories which were once believed to be true by a particular cultural group, and which served to explain (in terms of the intentions and actions of supernatural beings) why the world is as it is and things happen as they do, and to establish the rationale for social customs and observance and the sanctions for the rules by which men conduct their lives.[9]

Here the definition of myth by M.H. Abrams raises three points which are noteworthy – the hereditary character of myth; second, the belief of the particular cultural group; and the third, the importance of the super-human beings. The role of myth is triple-layered – ritualistic, totemic and archetypal, and according to Abrams, myths, generally, "involve rituals – prescribed forms of sacred ceremonials".[10] Therefore, the ritualistic myth necessitates the component of sacredness while the totemic elements focus on religio-cultural roots of man. Archetypal aspects of myth describe the primordial time, the fabled time of the 'beginnings'. Northrop Frye finds:

In terms of narrative, myth is the imitation of action here or at the conceivable limits of desire which means that myth is a structural literary pattern recurrent in literature.[11]

Sigmund Freud rose to mythical proportions in relation to the id, ego and superego paradigms which are projected as causal necessities of a repressed psyche. Jung on the contrary, confines himself to the activities and manipulations of the collective unconscious which projects itself in the world as myth, archetype, folklore, ritual and the rest. He believes that myths have the power to express inner reality of man's hidden world more accurately than the scientific discourses. They are like a sort of therapy which are meant for the problems of humanity and work like a barometer of human emotions which are going on in his unconscious world. In order to express his visionary experience, the creative writer uses certain images and forms which have existed from time immemorial and impressed him as possessing everlasting values. The question is how far the writer has been able to manipulate these inherited tendencies into a personalized mode of expression. C.G. Jung describes this problem in *Contributions to Analytical Psychology*:

> The man who speaks with primordial images speaks with a thousand tongues, he entrances and overpowers, while at the same time, he raises the idea he is trying to express above the occasional and the transitory into the sphere of the ever existing …
>
> Recoiling from the unsatisfying present, the yearning of the artist reaches out to that primordial images in the unconscious which is best fitted to compensate the insufficiency and one-sidedness of the spirit of the age. The artist seizes this image … transforming its shape, until it can be accepted by his contemporaries according to their powers.[12]

Max Muller finds myth as an expression of a "mutated language".[13] While according to Cassirer, "man's language which is the prime instrument of reason "reflects his myth-making tendency more than his rationalizing tendency."[14]

The major conflict lies in belief of man if it is 'myth' or

'reason', conscious or unconscious, truth and illusion. Levi Strauss believes:

> 'Reason' unlike 'Myth' is not man's primitive endowment but his achievement that the difference between, myth and language lies in the fact that myth never breaks out the magic circle of its figurative ideas, but the language born in the same magic circle has the power to break its bonds".[15]

Thus language and myth are the twins of human symbolic expressions. But Levi Strauss uses a scientific method to the expression of myth whereas Ernst Cassirer applies the Neo-Kantian attitude which is based on the spiritual reality of the mystical consciousness. Rejecting the allegorical significance of myth, Cassirer underlines that the mythological thinking is "theogonic process and the mythical figures are the autonomous configuration of human spirit."[16] He rejects Schelling's view that myths are transformed into history and establish the primitive attempts to explain nature. The philosophical understanding and the use of myth consists in the belief that myth is not a product of invention and imagination, "but a mode of necessity and therefore, in accordance with the idealist concept of the object, its own mode of reality."[17]

Therefore, it is not myth but the human consciousness which is an ocean of human experience and Cassirer rightly argues,

> Myth has no existence outside human consciousness, but even though mythological process consists solely in determination of consciousness – that is, in idea - this process, this success of representations, cannot have been merely represented as such but must have really taken place, must really have occurred in consciousness.[18]

In the mythological process, things edify the consciousness which holds a mind in its interior spaces. Apart from it, there is a fundamental difference between the mythic and the scientific imagination. The science requires logic and analysis with a touch of clarity which is perceptive to human mind like the light of day. The mythical imagination concentrates on the present, and the immediate present acquires a sort of religious significance which influences the human consciousness of people in the world. The reality of myth is not governed by the empirical and scientific laws but it has values of experience for the perceptive mind. Myth thus transcends the world of concrete spirituality into the mythical reality.

Myth is a process of identification which envelops the essence that incarnates itself into acts and facts. The range of a human consciousness involves history and pastness of past which finds expression in myth, that blends the social concerns of the present and the past. In the words of David Daiches, "the interest in archetypal patterns in poetry is often side by side with the interest in myth and the primitive mind."[19]

Myths have their origin in a certain cosmogony which exhibit not only how the world was created but also about how the world can be periodically regenerated, and how, consequently, a man can participate in this universal recreation. Harry M. Johnson is of the view, "Most myths have to do with the origins- the origin of gods, the world of culture, of certain features of nature. Other myths are stories of exploits of the gods or miraculous events in the lives of religious leaders."[20]

One can also witness other types of myth relating to

(a) the gods and of other divine beings,

(b) the creation of man,

(c) the subsequent modification of the world and of human conditions,

(d) the human beings of heroic grandeur and scale.

In the words of Rajesh K. Pallan: "Myth is an expression of man's deepest concerns about himself and his space in the scheme of the universe and that of his relationship with man, nature and god."[21]

It basically expresses the events which assess the relationships and privileges of important characters in building the contemporary ethos. Mythology thus becomes the living religion of a tribe and a guide to the psyche of man. Jung affirms that myths have a religious basis. They vindicate man's place in the universe, interpret human life, and serve as a record of human consciousness in contemporary contexts. Myths reveal the character and characteristics of different periods of cultural history where man is the protagonist. It is relevant to quote Northrop Frye when he considers,

> Myth is the central informing power that gives archetypal significance to ritual. It is the first verbal expression of literature and is an expression of the total vision of human situation."[22]

Frye finds out myth as the archetype, and the archetypal criticism cultivates an identity of the individual and the universal forms of images which are found in comedy and tragedy. He refers to the archetypal images relating to the human, animal, vegetable, mineral and that of the uniformed world which are well expressed in comedy and tragedy. In this context, it is relevant to quote Richard Chase who says,

> Literature becomes mythical by suffusing the natural with preternatural force towards certain ends, by capturing the impersonal forces of the world and directing them toward the fulfilment of certain emotional needs.[23]

One can also witness the typical forms of myth which according to Frye reveals,

> The typical forms of myth become the conventions and genres of literature. There are four main narrative genres – comedy, romance, tragedy and irony (satire) – and these are 'displaced' modes of the elemental forms of myth, associated with the seasonal cycles of spring, summer, autumn and winter.[24]

The roots of myth can be traced in history as every myth has, more or less, a true historical background. By continuous usages and inheritance, a myth expresses more and more the ideology of the society. Myths also highlight the problems of history, but because of its unavoidable inconsistency, no myth can prove a historical proof of facts. But we cannot deny the horrible facts of history like hunger, diseases and plagues faced by humanity in the past which the historical myth incorporates as the processes of continuity and revision of historical facts in the present. It is how myth develops and makes literature lively more than history. There is a process of continuity and connectivity from one generation to other. Thus tellers of history explain their own ideology, social class, or other factors which differ from one to the other. These processes connect time of past to the present as a revision. Myth keeps its main thrust of time in forms of ideas and ideologies which carry out the seeds of continuity in literature.

Myths serve as creative and functional frameworks for the creative writers who, then, discover schemata to evolve their work in. Aeschylus's *The Oresteion*, Virgil's the *Aeneid*, Dante's the *Divine Comedy*, Shakespeare's *A Mid Summer Night's Dream* and *the Tempest*, and John Milton's *Paradise Lost* are some of the remarkable examples where myths are abundantly and variously used. Modern writers like James Joyce in *Ulysses*, T.S. Eliot in *The Wasteland*, O'Neill in *Mourning Becomes Electra*, Melville in *Moby Dick* and many others have significantly woven their contemporary material on the mythic parallels. Hermann Hesse, Thomas Mann, Kafka, W.B. Yeats and D.H. Lawrence are some of the other prominent writers who have effectively used mythical and archetypal modes of expression in an age that has gone radical changes in terms of the system of values and the modes of living itself. The celebration of the bizarre and the absurd in the post World War second era has also discovered myth to be a valid mode of projection of contemporary issues.

Meenakshi Mukherjee points out that the conscious use of myth as a literary device is a modern trend. Such mythical method has been used by T.S. Eliot, James Joyce and O'Neill. They have consciously used "mythical situations and characters in a modern context, thereby seeking to illuminate the predicament of contemporary man, viewing him in a larger perspective of time".[25]

It is relevant to say that T.S. Eliot was deeply influenced by Jessie Weston's book *From Ritual to Romance* and James Frazer's famous book *The Golden Bough*. Weston's book supplied him the legend of the Grail and Fisher King, and from the *The Golden Bough* he was acquainted with a number of vegetation and fertility, myths and rituals. The myths of Adonis, Attis, Osiris and a countless drowned and hanged gods are described by James Frazer. Eliot discussed these ancient myths in *The Wasteland* as a part of his critical method of 'objective co-relative' for equating the human emotions. Eliot uses myth for a therapy for the spiritual wrecks and sustains the spiritual strength for spiritually barren contemporary society. While commenting on T.S. Eliot's use of Myth, Elizabeth Drew refers to the mythical method,

> ... that method of perceiving inner realities through their reflection in concrete image, and all the disciplines which have to accompany its translation into language, was what Eliot was in particular 'battling to recapture' in the practice of poetry[26].

The modern writer experiments with ancient myths and legends for explaining the facts of modern life, and in this way, co-relates the past with the present. He experiences the power of myth for constructing the variety, complexity and intricacy of modern life. Since the writer has to use a sense of the multiplicity of his age, he has to resort to some order and forms of literature. Modern writers particularly, T.S. Eliot and James Joyce, bring about such order and control by using the mythical method which 'involves a perception not only of the pastness of the past but also of the present'[27] as Eliot puts forth in a different context.

"Myth" for D.H. Lawrence "is an attempt to narrate a whole human experience of which the purpose is too deep, going too deep in the blood and soul, for mental explanation or description."[28] Thomas Mann links the past and the present with a frame of reference which maintains the structural unity in his works. In *Moby Dick*, Melville has imagined a significant story with responses originated from the unconscious world and which universalized the human emotions.

On the basis of the above discussions regarding myth, one can say that myths are the essential body of ideas of society. Mythic story expresses a spiritual truth or basic conviction of a culture through narrative. It expresses the impossibility of human efforts to attain the level of God. Myth is thus a key to the unity and identity of human emotions. While creating myths the creative writer shapes myth according to his artistic requirements which may vary from genre to genre. The relevance of myths in the study of literature is that myths and legends affect eternity.

Myth represents the culture of a country, its soul and amalgamates the past with the present which projects universality and timelessness into a work of art. Myths have been created by human beings for many reasons over thousand of years which are a superb product of humanity and a rich resource for the collective consciousness of mankind. Myths vividly describe customs, beliefs, attitudes of people and community and bring essential unity in diversity between the past and the present and develop the universal feelings of human pleasures and sufferings. Therefore, modern writers discover a principle of mythical patterns to sustain order and unity of the chaotic variety and complexity of the modern life. That is why myths and legends have become a favourite literary technique which is used quite frequently in literature.

Bringing out the deep relationship between myth and literature, Northrop Frye writes:

> Myth provides the main outlines and the circumference of a verbal universe which is later occupied by literature as well. Literature is more flexible than myth, and fills up the universe more completely; a poet or a novelist may work in areas of human life apparently remote from the shadowy gods and gigantic story – outlines of mythology. But in all cultures mythology merges intensibly into, and with literature.[29]

Frye further says,

> Myth and literature occupy the same verbal space, so to speak, the framework or context of any work of literature can be found in mythology as well, where its literary tradition is understood.[30]

Artistic and creative writers make use of myth according to the functional demands of the evolution of their creation. A particular use of myth is also necessitated by the kind of message the creative writer has in mind to deliver. Richard Chase has, therefore, emphasized the literary nature of myths. He observes that in the twenties and thirties, creative artists like W.B. Yeats, James Joyce, T.S. Eliot and a historian like Toynbee realized potentiality of the use of myth in literature and produced mythological literature. They feel that the first rate literature could be created with the juxtaposition of myth and mythic patterns for modern problems. He considers that writers are fascinated to myth primarily because it is literature itself. It is evident when he says, "Myth is literature, it has fictional character, which is imaginatively true."[31]

Science creates its own fiction and fictions evolve into myths of some kind or the other. Who can serve as a better example than H.G.Wells? Writers like D.H. Lawrence, T.S. Eliot, W.B. Yeats and James Joyce perceive the future literature in using myth as literature:

> Literature must be allied with myth. Somehow it is felt, the creative artist must recapture a certain magical quality, a richness of imagery, a deep sense of primeval forces a large order of aesthetic experience."[32]

Apart from poetry, the novel is one of the important genres of literature where relationship between myth and the novel is quite evident. Both are narratives prolonged in time and space. It is pertinent to quote Frye who finds myth as a rightful use in the thematic concerns of fiction:

> There are two broad visions of literary works which may be called the fictional and the thematic. The former comprises works of literature with internal characters, and includes novels, plays, narrative, poetry folk tales, and everything that tells a story ...[33]

William Golding's *Pincher Martin* is a flashback novel but a mythic story can never be in flashback. The novel can go backward and forward but its creative power runs from past to the present and from present to the future as we find in Shashi Tharoor's *The Great Indian Novel*. The technique and scope of the novel are wider than those of myths. The characters of myths are archetypal.

R.K. Narayan, an Indian novelist, remarks, "The mythic characters are prototypes and mould in which humanity is cast, and remain valid for all time."[34] Characters become representative voice while the characters in the novel are complex and intricate. D.S. Dewari questions about the historical and moral treatment in myth and writes,

> A myth is seldom historical and moral. It has a non-fictional status. Its narrative methods place little emphasis on literary authenticity. A myth describes the gods, goddess and demons who belong to an unearthly plane, while a novel is an account of the people inhabiting on this earth, existing in a particular age.[35]

Myths thus focus on man and his universe whereas novels deal with man as an individual or as a social being. A myth deals with the fundamental archetypal events and characters. The novel can present a tale of mythical story in the dimensional way while other genres of literature do not have such freedom to utilize such situations and events. A poem, for instance, can express only a fragment of myth like T.S. Eliot's *The Waste Land* but not like novels where novelists have used myths and legends effectively and largely.

Myth is man's desire to be better than what he is. This, in turn, produces a system of normativities that carry ethical implications for communities and nations. The sociological problems also have an outlet of expressions in novels with such great similarities. Myth also serves like an agent of supernatural calamities and which creates a whirlpool of problems that a man has to face in life. D. K. Lal rightly opines: "It is a fact that myth in literature has captured the imagination of creative artists in primitive as well as in modern times which projects the sufferings and predicaments of man."[36] It emerges as a powerful weapon of novelists which carves out their hidden potentialities.

Myth represents the soul and spirit of Indian psyche and for Indian people, religious myths constitute 'true history'. V.S. Naipaul therefore realized during his second visit to India:

> Religious myths touched every part of the land ... story within story, fable within fable: that was what people saw and felt in their bones. Those were the myths, about gods and heroes of the epics, that gave antiquity and wonder to the earth and people lived on.[37]

The earliest forms of narratives found in the *Puranas* can be considered as mythic narratives where a dialogue between an exponent and an inquirer is interspersed with the dialogues and observations of other individuals. If the epics treat the legendary actions of heroes as mortal men, the *Puranas* celebrate the powers and works of gods. But the most characteristic feature of the *Puranas* is that they are essentially diffused and expansive which deal with almost every topic of interest to mankind. Thus, there are philosophical speculations, theology, and mythology all combined in one within the narrative.

Indian fiction in English has its basis in myths, particularly Hindu mythology, originated from the cosmogonical myths of the *Rigveda*. The Harappa civilization of the Indus Valley, cultivated a goddess of the Great Mother, who appears to have passed into Hindu myth as Parvati, the consort of Shiva, later known as the divine Mother of the Universe.

The main deities in Hindu mythology are Vishnu and Shiva. Vishnu acts in his thirty-two 'avatars'. The chief of these 'avatars' were born as Rama and Krishna in the different ages. Rama is considered as a vegetation-god who is born to remove 'evil' by killing a terrible demon, the king of Lanka, Ravana. The battle between Rama and Ravana is really a battle between 'Dharma' and 'Adharma'. Rama's victory is the victory of 'Dharma' (good). It reflects the conflict between 'good' and 'evil' like morality play.

Myth of Krishna signifies the concept of love, ideal as well as physical. He is not only a great warrior but a great teacher-philosopher who in the *Bhagvad Gita* describes the whole organization of Earth to Arjun and preaches principles of life to the world. He like Rama, is an avatar to kill Kansa, the great evil-doer and the King of Mathura. As he grows up, he creates a world of love by infatuating 'Gopis', the divine milkmaids, especially Radha and he enjoys Raslila which expressed the power of love.

Shiva, like Krishna, is another avatar of creation and preservation of mortality. He is a symbol of erotic power – 'lingam' and Parvati as a symbol of 'yoni; or vulva. They have the power of creation. Shiva is not only the god of generative power and lord of the dance but he is also the guardian of mortality. Both Rama and Krishna are also the body of Shiva. Brahma, Vishnu and Mahesh (Shiva) are the trinity God of creation, destruction and preservation of mortality.

According to Chitra Sankaran,

> Hindu mythology occupies a singular position in world today. Perhaps what makes Hindu mythology so singular is that it seems to contain in essence that most vital property of myth – great antiquity combined with perpetual contemporaneity.[38]

Hindu mythology finds its fullest expression in the Indian epics like the *Ramayana*, the *Mahabharata*, the *Bhagvad Gita*, the *Vedas*, the *Upanishads*, the *Vishnu Purana*, the *Shiv Purana* and the *Durga Saptasati*. These Indian classics serve as a source of narrative models to Indian English novelists.

Rajesh K. Pallan is of the view that the Indian English novelists search and nourish their roots in their own past and discover the mythical patterns in the realm of timelessness and experience the immediate present.[39] The Indian creative writers have not derived their models of the use of myth from the writers in the West. This is as it should be because the magnitude and the variety of myths found in India is unparalleled. The stories of ancient Indian mythology thus have always been a source of inspiration to the Indian novelists in English.

Meenakshi Mukherjee writes in this connection:

> The Indian English novelists could benefit from the technical experiments of their European models, emulate their stream of consciousness method, or share their existentialist philosophy. But when they came to use myth in literature, they found that they could not draw their material from the

Greco-Roman or Judaeo-Christian mythical frame-work.[40]

It is not a difficult task for Indian English novelists to write on their Indian myths, "because Indian people", as Meenakshi Mukherjee writes, "are still closer to their mythology than the modern Irish or British people who are to Celtic folk-lore or Greek legends."[41] By juxtaposing mythic tales in their novels, the Indian novelists in English introduce profundity of meaning and the cultural milieu which brings the cosmological and the metaphysical significance in their works.

One can trace store-houses of the Hindu myths in the two great Indian epics the *Ramayana* and the *Mahabharata* and the *Puranas*. Every Hindu family in India has the book of The *Ramayana* and associates the events of Rama as a play of world drama in their life which signifies their contemporary relevance. The Indian mind is sensitive to perceive the significance of these myths and the stories of the *Ramayana*, the *Mahabharata*, *Panchtantra*, the *Puranas*, the *Upanishads* and the *Bhagvad Gita*. In this context it is apt to quote Jawaharlal Nehru when he says,

> I do not know of any books anywhere which have exercised such a continuous pervasive influence on the mass mind as these two – The *Ramayana* and the *Mahabharata*. Dating back to a remote antiquity, they are still a living force in the life of the Indian people.[42]

People of India who sustain the traditional culture accept myth as reality. In this respect Eliade explains:

> What does a living mean for a man who belongs to a traditional culture? Above all, it means living in accordance with extra-human models in conformity with archetypes. Hence it means living at the heart of the real since there is nothing truly real except the archetypes. Living in conformity with the archetypes amounted to respecting the 'law', since the law was only a primordial hierophany, the revelation in *illo tempore* of the norms of existence, a disclosure by a divinity or a mystical being.[43]

During 1930s most of Indian novelists started writing fiction in English and used myth in their novels. They looked into the realm of their past experience and brought out the contemporary reality in the clearer and meaningful way by associating the past experience with the present one. If English writers went to ancient myths and legends, juxtaposed them with the facts of modern life, and thus brought out the similarities and contraries between the past and the present, Indian novelists in English also discussed complexity and intricacy of modern life in their novels. The mythical method proved a viable tool to handle the complexity and chaos of modern life.

Eminent Indian novelists in English from the Pre-Independence period to the 60s, who used myths in their novels, are Mulk Raj Anand, Raja Rao, R.K. Narayan, Sudhindra Nath Ghosh and Bhabani Bhattacharya. The second generation which begins from 1970s to the present day, the novelists who used myths in their novels are Salman Rushdie, Anita Desai, Amitav Ghosh, Shashi Deshpande, Shashi Tharoor, Vikram Chandra and Sunny Singh. They skilfully counterpoint myth and modernity in their fiction.

For the Pre-Independent novelists like Raja Rao, R.K. Narayan and Sudhindra Nath Ghosh, myths used in their novels are based on Puranic narratives. Mulk Raj Anand is basically a social crusader and humanist critic. Many of his novels depict the topsy-turvy life of contemporary society, but his novel *The Old Woman and the Cow* draws a special attention in projecting life and society. It is a highly mythical novel which is replete with Sita myth. Anand has mastered his own design, dimension and dignity with which the novel is graced. All Indian-English novelists do not treat myths as analogies, but they make them their principal subject matter or structural principle. The two fundamental characteristics of such works are: first that the mythological parallel which is suggested as an analogy or contrast (as in the case of Mulk Raj Anand's *The Old Woman and the Cow*) to the contemporary world where many events occur in the novel; and second, that the parallel which is extended and described as a Radha-Krishna motif in Raja Rao's *The Serpent and the Rope*. According to Meenakshi Mukherjee, "There seems to be two distinct ways in which myths have been used in Indian English fiction: as a part of a disgressional technique of which Raja Rao is the most outstanding exponent and as structural parallels, where a mythical situation underlines the whole or a part of a novel."[44]

Both Raja Rao and Sudhindra Nath Ghosh have used myth in digressional manner in their novels. Sudhindra Nath Ghosh's novels *Cradle of the Clouds* (1951), *The Vermilion Boat* (1953) and *The Flame of the Forest* (1955) are replete with myths, legends and folklore.

Raja Rao has used myth in his novels regarding the ancient oral *Puranic* tradition of *Âkhyana*, which weaves the tangled webs of incidents in a literary manner. He makes the digressional use of myth in his novels *Kanthapura* (1938), *The Serpent and the Rope* (1960) and *The Cat and Shakespeare* (1965). His digressional technique can be associated with the ancient Indian technique of narration but his novels contextualize and mythologize contemporary reality. His fiction has a typical Indian ethos dipped into Indian classics which is found everywhere in his works. He has cravings of his own rich Indian past and correlates his mythical experience with the experience of the immediate present. His novels *Kanthapura*, *The Serpent and the Rope* and *The Cat and Shakespeare* reveal the philosophical themes of selfless action; self-knowledge and self-surrender which are treated as the three ways of deliverance from the bondage of life. Raja Rao perceives a vast panorama of human emotions and experience in the mythical perception in his novels, which establishes his distinctive quality as a novelist.

Kanthapura is a political and Gandhian novel which has localized myth. Moorthy of the village has become a local Gandhi and Kanthapura appears as a political battlefield of India. The village reminds us of the whole country. In the words of G.N. Agnihotri,

> Like the *Ramayana* and the *Mahabharata*, *Kanthapura* is an epic of Gandhism and the village. It is a novel of the higher order and it depicts with realistic details, a picture of the social, political and economic awakening which took place in the early decades in Indian villages.[45]

In *The Serpent and the Rope*, Ramaswamy's spiritual soul searching sufferings and his quest for self-realization remind us of Advaita Indian Philosophy. The search also parallels the search of Gautam Buddha for truth. The recurrent mythical allusion in the novel evokes the binary relationship of Radha-Krishna, Satyavan-Savitri, which designs the governing motif in the relationship between Ramaswamy and Madelaine. He craves for the mythical woman like Savitri who is committed to her husband. The Conflict of mythical woman and modern woman re-analyzes the importance of husband and wife relationship. The hero seeks his 'self' in the image of woman as wife in hers. It gives a typical identity of self in man and woman.

In *The Cat and Shakespeare*, Raja Rao has used the myth of hunter and the bilva tree. Myths like those of Sindbad, Hanuman and Bhima have also been used for creating mythical identity of characters. By employing myths in his novels, Raja Rao endeavours to create a belief that all human beings have similar feelings and all human experiences and human sufferings are identical.

Unlike Raja Rao and Sudhindra Ghosh, R.K. Narayan makes structural use of Myth in *The Man Eater of Malgudi* (1961) and myth in digressional manner specially in *Mr. Sampath* (1949), *The Painter of Signs* (1976) and *A Tiger for Malgudi* (1983).

R.K. Narayan has consciously sustained the use of myth and folklore in his novels where Myth and symbol emerge as the significant creative models for conveying a meaningful world-view of human drama as human reality as a part of shared human experience.

In *Swami and Friends*, the incident of launching a paper-boat with an ant-seated in it in a gutter is narrated in the Indian folklore. In *The Bachelor of Arts*, the depiction of the four stages in Chandran's life has a close parallel with ancient Hindu concept of four ashrams – *Brahmacharya*, *Grihastha*, *Vanaprastha* and *Sanyasa*. Savitri, in *The Dark Room*, bears a light echoes of Shakuntala and in her assertion of the right to live and die; her frightening encounter in the temple Shanti; and her own inescapable weakness not to live without the support of her family and home remind us of her mythical namesake leanings of characters in the past.

Mr. Sampath not only refers to India's remote past but it also introduces characters and stories from the Indian epics and the *Puranas* which took place in Malgudi. One can witness fantastically comic burning of Kama by Lord Shiva's Third eye in the novel.

In *The Financial Expert*, the novelist uses two symbols for gaining wealth, milk and lotus, which narrate the story of the rise and fall of the financial enchanter, Margayya. There are two contrary mythical symbols namely, Lakshmi and Saraswati, with their respective devotees in Margayya and Dr. Pal. Apart from it, there is a description of the myth of Markandya who wins death by the worshipping of Shiva. The mythical theme of the Goddess Agni, as the sacrificial agent, and the banyan tree, reminiscent of the tree of Lord Buddha's enlightenment, have also been used as a part of the Indian myth of Time and Chronology.

The use of Bhasmasura myth in *The Man Eater of Malgudi*, Santanu-Ganga legend in *The Painter of Signs* and Siddhartha's enlightenment in *A Tiger of Malgudi*, highlight R.K. Narayan as a myth-making novelist. The use of varied myths in fictional structures reveals the novelist's balanced vision of human life. In his novels there is a total religious involvement in which characters live and enjoy visiting temples and performing religious rituals. References of temples like Hanuman Temple, Laxmi Temple in *The Financial Expert* and the portrayal of Sanyasis in *The Dark Room*, the *Financial Expert*, *Bachelor of Arts* and *A Tiger for Malgudi* reveal his deep rooted faith in Hindu religion and that of Indian ethos.

Bhabani Bhattacharya's novels deal with the naked and horrible reality of his society. The novel *So Many Hungers* unfolds the story of hunger and starvation of the historical famine of Calcutta and Bengal. *He Who Rides a Tiger* records not only the misery and suffering of the poor but also the cruelty of the rich. It shows how the rulers of society grind and exploit the weak and the poor. The novel exposes religion as the baseless facts of life where starving people satisfy their soul in protecting their faith in the name of god and as a result, sacrifice everything to the temple where the protagonist of the novel, Kalo earns money. Bhattacharya has depicted it in the mythic framework which is governed by Kaliyuga. His *So Many Hungers* and *He Who Rides a Tiger* describe the post-independent India as the Kaliyuga of mythical India. *He Who Rides a Tiger* deals with the myth of Kali while *Music for Mohini* and *A Goddess Named Gold* are also mythically treated as his characters of the novels have mythical resemblances. Lachmi appears as Lakshmi, Meera Bai as Meera in his novel. *A Goddess for Gold* deals with the myth of goddess Lakshmi. *Shadow from Ladakh* is highly symbolical in which the novelist portrays political figures as the divine characters. Mahatma Gandhi and Pt. Nehru are carved out as men of high values. The novelist portrays them as gods because they possess god-like qualities.

Regarding the Post-Nehruvian era, Salman Rushdie, Anita Desai, Amitav Ghosh, Shashi Deshpande and Shashi Tharoor emerge as the representative novelists who used myths effectively in their novels for shaping the contemporary reality. Salman Rushdie's novels *Grimus*, *Midnight's Children*, *Shame* and *The Ground Beneath Her Feet* are of high eminence. *Grimus* contains Persian, Greek and Norse myths. In *Shame* Rushdie has created the myth of Sufiya Zinobia whereas *The Ground beneath Her Feet* is imbued with the Greek myths of Orpheus and Eurydice. In all these novels his use of myth depicts the contemporary against the universal.

Anita Desai's *Where Shall We Go This Summer* (1982) employs the major myth of Rama and Sita. Shashi Deshpande's *A Matter of Time* (1996) reflects myths from *Brhadaranyaka* Upanishad and *Katha Upanishad*. Amitav Ghosh's *The Circle of Reason* is a highly mythical novel which deals with the ancient Indian Upanishadic myth of Nachiketa. To Ghosh, mythical figures are the most suitable paradigms in order to explore and interpret the malady of modern ethos. Shashi Tharoor's *The Great Indian Novel* (1989) is a crucial commentary on the political history of modern India. The novel is modelled on the great Indian epic the *Mahabharata*. The contemporary Indian English novelists like Salman Rushdie, Amitav Ghosh, Anita Desai, Shashi Deshpande and Shashi Tharoor reinterpret contemporary socio-political history through the use of mythical figures. They represent the socio-political situations gaining ground in the post Nehruvian India which becomes the part of their post-colonial discourse. They project a new history in the light of mythical framework which decides their fate in the sands of time.

The contemporary fiction builds a timeless history in the light of mythical figures which ranges from ancient, medieval to modern age. History in contemporary novels is treated as a greater source of human consciousness. Therefore, the novelists like Rushdie, Amitav Ghosh and Shashi Tharoor present a 'perspective history' or a 'future history'.

Vikram Chandra's *Red Earth* and *Pouring Rain* (1995) is a parody of *Mahabharata* and *Arabian Nights*. Anjana Appachana's *Listening Now* (1998) is an interesting rewriting of the Shakuntala tale.

Sunny Singh's *Nani's Book of Suicides* (2000) explores the cultural history and identity of Indian women in the narratives which are rich in feelings and experiences expressed through the story of the family of modern India. As a typical Indian English novelist, Sunny Singh has used the stories of a number of mythological and legendary Indian women, which are woven into the structure of the novel. The narrator of the novel, Sammy makes frantic efforts to escape from the dark forces of which her Nani is an embodiment. Nani is the representative of the age-old traditions of the Hindus. Sunny becomes Sammy after undergoing 'Western incarnation' and gets transformed into diametrically opposite 'self'. Her efforts of freedom and liberation from shackles of traditions and honour of family prove futile and unworthy.

The novel records Sammy's memories of the past which are associated with her maternal grandmother at Banaras. She compares her present days with that of her childhood years of the past and she finds her past more fascinating and more captivating. Her memories always pursue her throughout in the world of the novel. She associates her with many mythical and legendary figures like Suniti, Draupadi and Kunti. Padmini, Kunti, Draupadi, Sita and

Meera of the past build Sammy's collective consciousness. The novelist considers it as a glowing tribute to the immortal Indian legendary women. In a way, it is a novel of Indian woman and for the woman.

Thus Indian English novelists have used myths in their novels in the distinctive manner and bring out the similarities and contrariness between the past and the present. Myth is a powerful literary device which helps the Indian English novelists to interpret modern India in the light of ancient mythical tradition. Myth also helps the contemporary writers for exploring their own existential concerns in the contemporary social context which makes their work good and durable.

The present study attempts to highlight the imaginative treatment of mythological incidents and situations which are discernable in Raja Rao's *The Serpent and The Rope* (1960), R.K. Narayan's *The Man Eater of Malgudi* (1961), Salman Rushdie's *Midnight's Children* (1981), Amitav Ghosh's *The Circle of Reason* (1986) and Shashi Tharoor's *The Great Indian Novel* (1989). The subsequent chapters will examine the varied use of myth in the novels undertaken for the present study.

REFERENCES

1 Cassell's *Encyclopedia of Literature*, Volume I. Ed. S.H. Steinberg (London : 1953), p. 327.

2 Mark Schorer: "The necessity of myth" in *Myth and Myth Making*, ed.A. Murray (Boston: Beacon Press, 1960), p. 355.

3 V. Rai: *Use of Myth in the Poetry of the Romantic Revival* (BHU: Unpublished Ph.D. Thesis), p.2.

4 P. Lal: "Myth and the Indian Writer in English : A Note" ed. M.K. Naik, *Aspects of Indian Writing in English* (Madras:Macmillan India, 1979), p. 15.

5 Mircea Eliade: *The Myth of Eternal Return*, tr. from the French by William R. Trask (England: Routlege and Keyan Paul Ltd. 1955), p.3.

6 Elizabeth Drew: *T.S. Eliot: The Design of His Poetry* (Delhi: Doaba House, 1970), p.2.

7 Malinouski: "The Concept of Myth and Ritual in Literature", ed. John Halloway, *Studies in Shakespeare's Major Tragedies* (London: Routlege and Kegan Paul, 1961), p.170.

8 Quoted by Romilla Thapar: *Ancient Indian Social History* (New Delhi: Orient Longman, 1978), p. 296.

9 M.H. Abrams: *A Glossary of Literary Terms* (Bangalore: Prism Books Pvt. Ltd., 1993), p. 122.

10 *Ibid.*

11 Northrop Frye: *Anatomy of Criticism: Four Essays* (Princeton: Princeton University Press, 1971), p. 30.

12 C.G. Jung: Contributions to Analytical Psychology, Trans HG and Carry F. Baynes (1928, rpt. London: Routledge and Kegan Paul, 1948), p. 248.

13 Friedrich Max Muller: *Comparative Mythology*, reprinted in *Selected Essays on Language, Mythology and Religion* (London: George Routlege, 1909), pp. 299-300.

14 Ernst Cassirer: *The Philosophy of Symbolic Forms*, Vol. 2, *Mythical Thought*, trans. Ralph Manheim (New Haven: Yale University Press, 1957), p. 3.

15 Claude Levi-Strauss: *Mythologies*, trans. Rondley Needham (London: Merlin Press, 1964), p. 7.

16 Ernst Cassiner: *The Philosophy of Symbolic Forms*, Vol. 2, *Mythical Thought*, trans. Ralph Manheim (New Haven: Yale University Press, 1957), p. 4.

17 *Ibid.*, p. 4.

18 *Ibid.*, p. 6.

19 David Daiches: *Critical Approaches to Literature* (Bombay: Orient Longman, 1973), p. 357.

20 Harry M. Johnson: *Sociology: A Systematic Introduction* (New Delhi: Allied Publishers, 1980), p. 405.

21 Rajesh K.Pallan: *Myths and Symbols in Raja Rao and R.K.Narayan* (Jalandhar: A B S Publications,1994), p. 8.

22 Northrop Frye: "The Archetypes of Literature", *Twentieth Century Criticism Major Statement*, ed. William J. Handy and Max Westbrook (New Delhi: Light and Life Publishers, 1974), p. 240.

23 Richard Chase: "Notes on the Study of Myth", *Twentieth Century Criticism: The Major Statement*. Ed. William J. Handy and Max Westbrook (New Delhi: Light and Life Publishers, 1974), p. 248.

24 Northrop Frye; *op. cit.*, p. 158

25 Meenakshi Mukherjee: *The Twice Born Fiction* (Delhi: Arnold Heinemann Publishers (India) Pvt. Ltd., 1974), p. 128.

26 Elizabeth Drew: *T.S. Eliot: The Design of His Poetry* (Delhi: Doaba House, 1970), p. 14.

27 T.S. Eliot: "Traditon and the Individual Talent", *Twentieth Century Criticism: The Major Statements* ed. William J. Handy and Max Westbrook, p. 29.

28 D.H. Lawrence: "The Dragon of the Apocalypse", *Selected Literary Criticism*, ed. A. Beal, (Mercury Books), p. 158.

29 Northrop Frye: "Myth, Fiction and Displacement", *Twentieth Century Criticism: The Major Statements*, p. 165.

30 *Ibid.*, p. 168.

31 Richard Chase: "Foreword", *Quest for Myth* (New York: Greewood Press, 1969), p. vi.

32 *Ibid.*, p. 110.

33 Northrop Frye: *Twentieth Century Criticism: The Major Statements*, p. 156.

34 R.K. Narayan: *Gods, Demons and Others* (Mysore : Indian Though Publications, 1973), p. 4.

35 D.S. Dewari: *The Use of Myth in R.K. Narayan's Novels* (New Delhi: Prestige Books, 2001), p. 13.

36 D.K.Lal: *Myth and Mythical concepts in O'Neill's Plays*,(New Delhi: Atlantic Publishers and Distributers,1992), p.32

37 V.S. Naipaul: *India A Million Mutinies Now* (London: Minerva, 1990), p. 144.

38 Chitra Sankaran: *The Myth Connection* (New Delhi: Allied Publishers Ltd. 1993), p. 2.

39 Rajesh K.Pallan: *op. cit.*, p. 17.

40 Meenakshi Mukherjee; op. cit., p. 15.

41 *Ibid.*, p. 16.

42 Jawaharlal Nehru: *The Discovery of India* (New Delhi: Oxford University,1974), p. 99.

43 Mircea Eliade: *The Myth of Eternal Return*, tr. from French by William R. Trask, p. 95.

44 Meenakshi Mukherjee; *op. cit.*, p. 137.

45 G.N. Agnihotri: "Raja Rao – The Distinguished Philosopher – Novelist", *Indian Life and Problems in the Novels of Mulk Raj Anand, Raja Rao and R.K. Narayan* (Meerut: Shalabh Prakashan, 1993), p. 80.

2

The Serpent and the Rope: Mythic Dimensions

Raja Rao, one of the Big Three of Indo-Anglian fiction of the first generation, has been the literary master of myth-making in Indian writing in English. His fiction is a monument of Indian thought and culture. He delves deep into myths, folklores, fables, and religions of India. He incorporates idealism as a part of human reality, and has transformed the turmoil of the age into the finer spiritual stirrings. He has converted his *Kanthapura*, a novel of national movement into a veritable 'Sthalapurana' emanated from the Puranas. The village becomes a microcosm of the macrocosm of national movement.

The chapter opens with Raja Rao's novel *Kanthapura* preceding the publication of *The Serpent and the Rope*. This helps to evolve a perspective in the light of the psyche of the novelist who has creatively expressed thousands of years old Indian philosophical and mythological traditions. The subsequent part of the chapter would be devoted to a study of *The Serpent and the Rope* as constituting a mythological structure with philosophical implications.

Raja Rao was influenced by authors and books of India especially the *Ramayana* which "has influenced me most, as it has every Indian. The book has filled my imagination and come to me for years at every crucial point of my life, to interpret and to help"[1]. He is also deeply influenced by the *Mahabharata*. The *Ramayana* and the *Mahabharata* constitute the bedrock of Indian intellectual culture. Apart from it, Raja Rao's works have a typical

Indian ethos and ancient Indian classics like the *Vedas*, the *Puranas*, the *Upanishads*, the *Bhagvad Gita* etc. have helped him in understanding the spirit of India. He can only think in terms of Indian consciousness which has been the root of Indian culture.

His moorings of Indian past were translated into mythic experiences as connected with the immediate present. His works appear like a replica of Indian scriptures that we can find in the *Puranas*, the *Vedas* and the epics.

In his interview with Shiva Niranjan, Raja Rao admits:

I like to write a Purana. I like the Puranic conception, in fact, that is the only conception of novel for me. I don't want to write like a foreign novelist. I am very much an Indian and the Indian form is the Puranic form.[2]

Raja Rao is also a great admirer of the great American 'triumvirate' – Ralph Waldo Emerson, Henry David Thoreau and Walt Whitman because of their spiritual learning that they found in the philosophy of India. He also admires those Americans who read Plato, Aristotle and Cicero. Rao's attitude towards life is much elevated and laden with philosophical insights which are sublimated beyond any degree. He is a great lover of truth because truth is God to him like Mahatma Gandhi. In *The Serpent and the Rope*, he compares truth with Brahminism. True Brahmin is an idol of God on the earth and he continues this Brahminic tradition in the novel.

He has used myths which can be categorized into three parts:

(i) Puranic Myths

(ii) Localised Myths

(iii) Rites and Rituals-related Myths

The Puranic myths pertain the binary trends which can be seen as 'good' in opposite with the evil and war between Rama and Ravana becomes a symbolic war between 'good' and 'evil'. The myth in *Kanthapura* is a war between Rama and Ravana and also between Gandhi and the British rule. The Gandhian army of freedom fighters comes forth as the brutal force before the army of the Red Man. By using Indian myth for Time and Chronology, and by mythologizing the historical characters, the novelist has telescoped myth as a path-maker of past and the present which goes forward towards the future.

Raja Rao uses the Gandhian context of 'Selfless action' in *Kanthapura* which leads to, 'Self knowledge' in *The Serpent and the Rope* and 'Self surrender' in *The Cat and Shakespeare*.

Rao's novel *Kanthapura*[3] (1938) is a novel about the freedom movement of India. It was a time of doubt and despair, but under the leadership of Mahatma Gandhi the whole nation had risen into a big non-violent army. People could not understand the spirit of Gandhi's philosophy but they came to know that he stood for the uplift of the poor and the untouchables. Like other villages of India Kanthapura also came under the impact of dynamic and benign guidance of Mahatma Gandhi.

The movement gathered momentum and almost the whole village got ready to offer passive resistance and suffer humiliation and blows to press demands. Agents of the British Government like Bade Khan and his associates were hurdles in the way of the Satyagrahis. But the protagonist of the novel Moorthy and his active associate Ratna did not mind their atrocious statements and harmful activities. As an ardent admirer of Mahatma Gandhi, Raja Rao has woven the tapestry of unconventional views of people in the texture of the novel *Kanthapura*.

According to M.K.Naik, "*Kanthapura* has the Puranic strain of philosophy harnessed to a predominantly religious world view[4]. The novel is a fictional rendering of '*Sthala – Purana*' - the legendary history of a place in the village. The localized myths are embedded in Goddess Kenchamma and her daughter river, Himavathy. The well-known epic or puranic myths are also revitalized in the novel as it dramatizes the philosophy of selfless action as explained in the *Bhagavad Gita*.

The Indian struggle for freedom is equated with the great war of *Mahabharata* in *Kanthapura* where Kenchamma appears like a veritable Krishna of Kurukshetra as a source of inspiration for war against the evil doer enemies. The novelist has even mythologized the historical characters like Mahatma Gandhi for enacting the war between the forces of good and evil, truth and untruth, love and hatred. The contemporary Indian reality of freedom struggle in a small village is telescoped by using myths for the cultural experiences of the Puranic world. The various myths in the novel reflect the whole ethos of Indian villages. In the Preface of *Kanthapura*, Raja Rao has pointed out the mythical context hidden in the novel with a touch of community consciousness which appears to be the Indian consciousness of past and present in the country:

> There is no village in India, however mean, that has not a rich sthala Purana, or a legendary history of its own. Some god or god-like hero has passed by the village – Ram might have rested under this Pipal tree. Sita might have dried clothes, after her bath on this yellow stone, or the Mahatma himself, on one of his many pilgrimages throughout the country, might have slept in this hut, the low one, by the village gate.[5]

Mahatma Gandhi thus becomes the incarnation of Lord Rama and Lord Krishna and as an *avatar*, he liberates Mother India from the tyrannical rule of Englishmen. Gandhi's character in *Kanthapura* has become as an idealized myth like that of Rama in the *Ramayana*. Mahatma Gandhi is not only compared with Rama, Krishna and Shiva but also with Raja Harishchandra, who has been an exponent and a martyr of truth. The King of Varanasi, Harishchandra, became a living legend of Truth and Honesty and, thus, became a mythical character.

In an interview with R. Parthasarthy, Raja Rao rightly remarks,

I think I try to belong to the great Indian tradition of the past when literature was considered a Sadhana.[6]

Like *Kanthapura*, *The Serpent and the Rope* (1960)[7] is also based on the Puranic pattern which is also episodic and digressional in approach. It is a philosophical novel which reveals the oriental characteristics of India and C.D. Narasimhaiah truly calls it as a novel of Indian sensibility:

> I felt a sudden thrill that here at last was the finest and fullest possible expression of an essentially Indian sensibility. The novel is acknowledged a classic of our time.[8]

Raja Rao has successfully portrayed the Indian ethos in his novel which symbolizes a journey from temporality to a transcendental order. The western narrative falls short of liberational ends and there is no deliverance there as it is in the Indian tradition. Ancient India is not the modern India with flourishing economy and the industrial growth in clusters but it is the age-old India with her feudalism, traditions, rituals, and landscapes of the sacred snows and rivers of mountains which got expression in the novel. There prevails an ardent quest for truth in the novel with numerous interpolated beautiful stories within the central story in the style of the *Mahabharata*. A number of legends, episodes and tediously long succession of digressions have also been used to point out the questions of moral in the novel. Through this novel Raja Rao seeks to convey the Advaitic philosophy of the 'oneness of all', the identity of 'Jiva' and 'Shiva' forms, which is centralized in the novel. Chitra Sankaran finds out philosophical and mythological dimensions in the novel as the "complex and intricate relationship with Hindu tradition which make the novel most problematic."[9]

In order to analyse the extensive and intensive use of myth in the novel, it is essential to discuss the theme of the novel in brief, which will help in locating the use of myth:

The narrator Ramaswamy is the central figure in the novel. He is a young and educated man who belongs to a rich landlord family of South India. He is an M.A. in history, and, on government scholarship, goes to France in order to carry on his research work and earn the Doctorate degree of the University of Sorbonne. There he meets Madeleine, a young French lady and a teacher at one of the University Colleges and falls in love with her. They are soon married and live happily together in Axis near Paris. A son is born to them, but, unfortunately he dies within a short span of time which provides a great shock to Madeleine, and she could not live to her usual self again. Madeleine, like Ramaswamy, is also interested in philosophy and religion, and, often, the philosophical discussions between them go on.

When Ramaswamy was in Europe for about a year, his father died, he was in hurry to comeback home. He carries Little Mother (the third wife of his father) and his baby brother, Sridhara, to Benares for the last rites of his father. From Benares they go over to Allahabad where they stay for sometime with an old friend of Rama's father. There he meets Pratap Singh who is betrothed to Savithri, the young Western educated daughter of the Raja of Surajpur. She does not want to marry him. Rama is fascinated by Savithri. From Allahabad they go to Hardwar and then return to their home. Rama has two sisters – Saroja and Sukmari. Saroja, a young educated lady of progressive views, is dissatisfied with the conventional and orthodoxical trends of the members of her family. She longs for the freedom like that of the West. Rama is influenced by her qualities of womanhood and regards her as the embodiment of the Feminine principle.

Having settled ritualistic affairs at home, Ramaswamy returns to France in order to complete his thesis which it is expected to take more than one year. Savithri also comes on a short visit to Cambridge on her way from India. Ramaswamy also visits Cambridge in connection with his research work, and comes in close contact with Savithri and passes many evenings together. He is passionately in love with her but thinks of Madeleine while in relationship with Savithri. Savithri eventually marries Pratap Singh and Ramaswamy comes back to Madeleine. He finds a great change in her as she became a devout Buddhist and is practising the eight-fold path of the Lord Buddha. She keeps fasts, and passes most of her time in prayer and meditation. Such religious determination and practice has generated a sense of isolation which leads to their separation.

However, they live together for sometime more. Then Ramaswamy goes to London for certain thesis references. He falls ill there and is hospitalized, and one of his lungs has to be taken out. Savithri who is in London for the Coronation of the Young Queen frequently visits him. On his discharge from the hospital, he comes to Paris, takes apartment there for, seclusion so that, he may write his thesis. He visits Madeleine and comes to know that she has become a 'Sanyasini' and they are ultimately divorced.

After the research work is over, he plans to go to Travancore in search of 'Guru'.

M.K. Naik rightly observes:

> *The Serpent and the Rope* is a highly complex and many-sided work of art, being at once the tragic story of a marriage of minds which drift apart; the spiritual autobiography of a learned sensitive, and imaginative modern Indian intellectual – and a saga of his quest for self-knowledge and self-fulfilment; a memorable statement of the prime values of both the East and the West and a drama enacting their mutual impact; a sustained piece of symbolism and a re-creation of a valuable ancient Hindu myth; and a conscious attempt both to create a truly Indian novel with its roots firmly embedded in native tradition and to forge an Indian English style through which alone could its complex vision be authentically and adequately presented.[10]

In *The Serpent and the Rope*, Raja Rao is the first novelist to attempt Indian mysticism and Vedantic philosophy as a subject of his novel. In *The Serpent and the Rope*, the 'Serpent' and the 'Rope' are the symbols of Illusion and Reality in the Indian intellectual tradition that Raja Rao weaves into the framework of his novel as ideas regarding 'illusion' and 'reality'. In the novel, Ramaswamy is an intellectual pilgrim who is yearning to seek truth into things and tries to understand the meaning and purpose of life. *The Serpent and the Rope* is also an excellent example of the fusion and conflict of the motifs of the East and the West, the Oriental and the Occidental, which makes the brilliant design of the novel. Meenakshi Mukherjee rightly comments:

> In Raja Rao's *The Serpent and the Rope*, the East-West theme assumes a depth and validity not achieved before in Indo-Anglian fiction. Here East, however, is no general term. It is India, Brahmanical India, which represents the quintessence of adavaita philosophy.[11]

The novel is not a book but an artistic vision of texts of Hindu philosophy. Ramaswamy represents the Upanishadic and Vedantic traditions and often discusses about his quest as a protagonist in framework of the novel. But the theme is a journey of spiritual quest which is of primary significance in the novel. Ramaswamy's quest for truth also becomes the quest of the author himself. O.P. Mathur appropriately calls that, "The novel is both a discovery of India and a discovery of the self"[12]. Such discovery of truth becomes the theme of the novel which is fully projected in a mythic framework and is laden with myths.

The Indianness of Raja Rao is marked out in a number of Indian myths and legends which are woven into the fabric of the novel. In the novel, myths and legends not only establish a link between the contemporaneity and antiquity but also substantiate and concretize the spiritual exploration of Ramaswamy. The novelist's art of narration is typically Indian. It is taken from the method of the Hindu *Puranas* which is a unique blend of history, literature, philosophy and religion, and encyclopedic presentation of the total human existence.

The myths of Radha-Krishna, Savithri-Satyavan and Iseult-Tristan play a vital role in constituting a spiritual meaningfulness between Savithri and Ramaswamy; and these mythic figures highlight the human relationship in the spiritual contexts. Although the central myth spreading through the novel is that of Radha and Krishna, yet there are other myths of Buddha, which symbolize in Ramaswamy's quest for self-realization. The failure of Rama's marriage to Madeleine is depicted on the mythical plane showing that womanhood is not fundamentally based upon the materialistic physical relationship but upon the spiritual meanings. In Indian mythology, woman is conceived as Shakti and woman appears as the mythical counterpart of man. Therefore, Raja Rao refers to the mythological characters like Satyavan's Savithri of the *Mahabharata* (p. 360); Rama's Sita of the *Ramayana* and that of the Rajput Princess "Mira, the poetess" (p. 43) whose 'Kanhayya' (beloved) is Lord Krishna, as manifestations of metaphysical truth (p. 35). It is suggested that womanhood is a vital entity which is complementary to Ramaswamy and also essential for his spiritual development. These metaphysical concepts were discussed thousands of years ago by the Upanishadic sages on the bank of the Ganges where *Rishis* have discussed the myth of Benares as a city of the Metaphysical understanding:

> I was the Pagan, in fact, going down the Ganges, feeling such worship for this grave and knowing river. Flowers floated down-stream, and now and again we hit against a fish or log of wood. Sometimes too a burnt piece of fuel from some funeral pyre would hit against the oars of the boat. People say there are crocodiles in the Ganges, and some add that bits of dead bodies, only half-burnt, are often washed down by the river. But I have never seen these myself. Night, a rare and immediate night, was covering the vast expanses of the Benares sky. Somewhere on these very banks the Upanishadic sages, perhaps four, five or six thousand years ago, had discussed the roots of human understanding". (pp. 23-24).

In another context, the husband and wife relationship is considered as a marriage of 'self' which is based on the Advaitic philosophy of 'one for all'.

Yagnavalkya had said to Maitreyi, "For whose sake, verily, does a husband love his wife? Not for the sake of his wife, but verily for the sake of the self in her." (p. 24).

It is the above assertion, Ramaswamy is convinced that his love for Madeleine is "for the sake of the self in her" and he realizes later on the metaphysical meaning of love. In a London hotel room, Savithri too realizes their symbolic and metaphysical context of love and Ramaswamy identifies the Feminine Principle (Savithri) in her for gaining a true perspective of his quest for wholeness.

Both Savithri and Ramaswamy achieve self-realization, where the Masculine Principle is greatly fused with the Feminine Principle. On the other hand, the marriage of Ramaswamy and Madeleine proves unsuccessful because Madeleine fails to follow the true Feminine Principle which conceptualises the feminine active principle, the material cause of the universe; the Maya that evolves the differentiated elements and being. The coronation of the Queen in the novel is also suggestive of the "apotheosis of the Feminine Principle"[13].

During his recuperation after the lung-operation, Ramaswamy contemplates on the coronation of Queen Elizabeth, the figures of the queen meeting, Rama and Savithri come to terms with the merges into that of Savithri in his consciousness. In their last meeting, Rama and Savithri come to terms with the real nature of their relationship and Rama calls her "my queen" (p. 364):

> "And what shall one do with one's pain?"
>
> "Know that to have pain is to give pain. Rejoice, Savithri Rejoice in the rejoicement of others. That is the truth."
>
> "You ask toc much, my love. Can I still call you that?"
>
> "Yes, my Principle, my Queen, you can. Love is rejoicing in the rejoicing of the other."
>
> "She touched me with the tip of her lips as though Truth had been there, just there, and the moment was the whole Truth". (p. 364)

The Feminine Principle, through which Ramaswamy recognizes the ultimate Truth, becomes "the touchstone for measuring the truth and falsity of philosophies, political systems, ideologies, people"[14]. Ramaswamy's quest for truth on the Feminine Principle is also multi layered that we can witness in his relationship with different women in varied forms – Madeleine, Savithri, Saroja, Lakshmi Little Mother and Aunt Lakshmana. (p. 170). According to the Indian mythology, Shakti is the active creative ideal and Heinrich Zimmer interprets thus:

> Maya-Shakti is personified as the world-protecting, feminine, maternal side of the ultimate being, and as such, stands for the spontaneous loving acceptance of life's tangible reality. She is the creative joy of life ... she instills into us – and she is herself – surrender to changing aspects of existence. Maya Shakti is Even, The Eternal Feminine[15].

Now in the novel, the Universe expresses the network of Maya. Ramaswamy's deep thought on womanhood are evident in lines when he says:

> Woman is the earth, air, ether, sound; woman is the microcosm of the mind, the articulation of space, the knowledge in knowledge; the woman is fire, movement clear and rapid as the mountain stream; the woman is that which seeks against that which is sought. To Mitra she is Varuna, to Indra she is Agni, to Rama she is Sita, to Krishna she is Radha. Woman is the meaning of the world. Woman is Kingdom solitude, time ... Woman is death, for it is through woman that one is born; Woman rules, for it is she, the universe. She is the daughter of the earth ... woman is the duality made for her own pools of mirroring and she crowns herself to show that man is not of this kingdom ... woman is the world. (pp. 352-353).

'Maya-Shakti' concept runs throughout the novel and forms an intrinsic part of the artistic pattern of the Advaitic philosophy inherent in the analogy as 'the serpent' and 'the rope', illusion and reality, Maya and truth.

The mythical parallels have been beautifully suggested in relationship between Savithri and Ramaswamy. Savithri in the novel bears the echoes of the mythical Savithri, wife of Satyavan, who married Satyavan knowing well that her husband is destined to live for one year more. When on the appointed day, Yama appears to take away the soul of Satyavan, Savithri follows him, always insisting on having the life of her husband restored. Ultimately, she succeeds in bringing back the soul of her husband to this earth.[16]

Savithri, in the novel, follows the same precedents as set by the great epic ladies like Sita and Savithri whose names are synonymous with wifely love and devotion. It is in his relationship with Savithri that Ramaswamy realizes the appropriate path for his quest for the Ultimate Truth. Her love for Ramaswamy is aesthetic as well as intellectual in nature for which the fulfilment of the physical passion is not so important as the gratification of soul. Savithri, like her mythical counterpart, emerges triumphant in leading her eternal love to the path of the knowledge of the self. She symbolizes love and the power of devotion which can conquer death itself. Madeleine represents death for Ramaswamy because her relationship with him happen to be merely on the physical level. In Savithri-Satyavan myth, Satyavan is revived after his death by the sincere efforts of his wife. In the similar vein, Madeleine whose both babies die in infancy, represents death for Rama. And it is she who unknowingly helps Rama achieve his mission of life by her own conversion to Buddhism. "Nowadays I rise like a good Buddhist at dawn, wash and say my mantras. My Buddhas are kind: the early morning meditations are wonderful ... 'Good night, Rama, she said at the door,' and sleep well. 'Worry is of the mind', says the Buddhist text. Do not worry, mon ami." (pp. 301-302). Her failure as a wife is Rama's success as a pilgrim's metaphysical progress.

The Radha-Krishna myth is a governing motif in the novel, which intensifies the spiritual relationship between Savithri and Ramaswamy. Savithri's love for Ramaswamy dramatizes the myth of the eternal love of Radha and Krishna. To Rama, Savithri is symbolic of Parvati and Radha; to Savithri, Rama is the symbol of Shiva and Lord Krishna. In the passage, Raja Rao describes Savithri's longing and devotion for Rama:

> A Hindu woman knows how to worship her Krishna, her lord. When the moon shines over the Jumna and lights are lit in the households, and the cows are milked, then it is Janaki's son plays on the banks of the Yamuna in Brindavan. The cattle tear their ropes away, the deer leave the forests and come leaping to the groves, and with the peacocks seated on the branches of the asoka, Krishna dances on the read earth. What gopi, my Lord, would not go to this festival of love? Women lose their shame and men rose their anger, for in Brindavan Krishna and Lord dances. (p. 209).

Savithri's ritual marriage to Rama signifies the union of the

Feminine Principle with the Masculine Principle. She comes to him in his hotel room in London and performs a mystic marriage. She washes her feet and sobs with love and Ramaswamy, in turn, coloured her head with 'Kumkum' and gives her coconut and beetle nuts that Ramaswamy described as her devotion to him:

> She knelt before me, removed one by one my slippers and my stockings and put them aside gently-distantly. She took flower and Kumkum, and mumbling some song to herself, anointed my feet with them'. Now she lit a camphor and placing the censer in the middle of the kumkum-water she waved the flame before my face, once, twice and three times in arathi. After this she touched my feet with the water, and made aspersions of it over her head, kneeling again and placing her head on my feet, she stayed there long, very long, with her breath breaking, into gentle sobs ... I have known my Lord for a thousand lives, from Janam to Janam have I known my Krishna ... (pp. 211-212).

Ramaswamy is reminded of the moving myth of Radha and Krishna which reveals man's endeavour to recognize the Absolute or the Super Self so he cannot marry the real Savithri, a soul. That is why he is satisfied with the mystic marriage to Savithri which means more than Savithri's marriage to Pratap. Ramaswamy takes a promise from Savithri to go back to India and be a good wife to Pratap. The conversation between Rama and Savithri reveals Radha-Krishna motif:

> "Oh, the world should never have learnt men like you". She repeated, "not stick. The world should be gay like the people at the Parc des Princes, play while you play and work while you work. Do you know Monte Carlo, Monsieur? She asked, "There you have so much sunshine that you want to loose all the birds from the cages."
>
> Madame Chimaye had one enemy. It was the man who did business with birds opposite. She hated him more than she hated the Americans. This man had Parks, parakeets, canaries ... and he sold grain for them, and medicine for the birds he sold too. He also made lovely cages – "These are the

> cages of Pekin ..." you could imprison your birds in lacquer, steel or oak, it all depended upon your purse and taste." (pp. 367-368).

Myths can go to spiritual ends as in the case of Krishna for whom Gopies abandoned their household duties creating problem in the process. Ramaswamy, therefore, advises Savithri to discover love within a scheme of symbolical relationships that do not transcend themselves. Ramaswamy knows that Savithri is a married lady and it is her duty to regard Pratap's house as her Brindavan, the garden associated with Lord Krishna and Radha for their love-making. He advised her to remain satisfied like his several gopis who were advised by Lord Krishna. He makes her realize the truth, and tells her:

> "Rama, I have a question."
> "Yes, Savithri? What is it?"
> "To whom does one belong?"
> "To one's self, Savithri."
> "What shall become of her that does not belong to herself?"
> "Then must she belong to someone."
> "But if she belong to one wholly, or rather almost wholely, and to another she be tied, as a calf is tied to the tether, or as the plane is tied to the radar."
> "The plane must accept the direction of the radar, that there be no accident. Either you are a plane and you follow national and international conventions – or you do not fly." (p. 363).

Ramaswamy advises her further:

> "Know that to have pain is to give pain.
>
> Rejoice, Savithri! Rejoice in the rejoicement of the others. That is the Truth ... Love is rejoicing in the rejoicing of the other". (p. 364).

Savithri recognizes her 'Dharma' to be Pratap's wife, as in the spiritual context, Sita is Rama's wife and as Radha is married to her Krishna. Her relationship with Rama is on a spiritual plane. She should be like the river Ganges who even after receiving all kinds of impurities, remains pure.

Rama's contact with Savitri generates in him a new meaning and awareness of 'self'. He is now capable of understanding the rhythm and meaning of mythical and metaphysical history through her. He develops a perfect understanding of the Feminine Principle that one can destroy one's ego in order to transcend one's self, and can achieve self-realization. After her symbolic marriage in a London hotel room, Savithri says to Rama: "I'will come when you do not need me". (p. 211). Thus their marriage becomes a fusion of two metaphysical souls for achieving the Ultimate Truth which shows that both are married to a higher ideal where self of individual is highlighted. Sexual love is considered as a self-forgetful devotion of metaphysical union of two loving 'selves'. Thus womanhood becomes a symbol for the spiritual making of the individual, and according to Ramaswamy, the concept of womanhood provides an awareness of the Oneness of Truth as a part of Advaitic philosophy. Rama thinks that "Man sees himself in woman as essence, the fact of womanhood is the meaning of his life. If there were nothing other, you could not know that you are." (p. 170). Without love for women, there could be no urge for Truth as it is a source of the awareness of self in the world. Stephen Hemenway writes in this context:

> Rama's search for women is one with his quest for self-knowledge. Both demand the death of illusion and the realization that the seeming many are one; both climax in a revelation of Truth.[17]

Such reverence and search for self in women makes Rama realize his spiritual Oneness in Savithri who firmly believes that man finds his expansion of self in his woman which causes the deep love of man for woman. Such relationship is both erotic as well as metaphysical that D.S. Mani considers that "in one sense, *The Serpent and the Rope* is a long and passionate plea for understanding the erotic base of all our spirituality"[18].

Madeleine loves Ramaswamy deeply and devotedly and he too responds with all his being - yet their marriage is a failure. Various reasons have been marked out for this failure. First, a woman seeks fulfilment in motherhood which was denied to her.

Their first child, a son, whom they named Krishna, died soon after birth which caused her a deep psychological injury. She could never recover the same nature of a carefree girl. The death of her second child gave her a traumatic shock in the psychological sense through which she could never recover. She developed a negative attitude, a detestation for worldly life, which culminated in her Buddhist renunciation and asceticism. Moreover, despite all her love for Ramaswamy she never participated in his inner self.

Unlike Savithri, Madeleine fails to understand the metaphysical meaning of the bond of marriage which is the essence of Rama's life. Both differ from each other in their perspectives. Madeleine regards Benares as an obnoxious city with its "bits of floating human flesh and pyres of the dead." (p. 39), while to Ramaswamy, the eternal "City is where Lord Shiva is worshipped as the great saviour in our voyage across the world, The blue-throated, the three eyer grantor of all desires ... The imperishable one." (p. 22). The conflict here is both ideological as well as metaphysical.

Just as Lord Krishna's wives – Satyabhama and Rukmini – failed to constitute a spiritual bond with Krishna like Radha, similarly, Madeleine could not rise to the level of spiritual love of Ramaswamy where physical marriage does not matter to the spiritual union of self. Her association with Rama becomes sterile and futile. She could not become the non-dual like Savithri and rejected marriage as a sacrament. She even regards mere touch as unholy. Rama describes her such outlook:

> Touch was always distasteful to her. So she liked the untouching Cathars, she loved their celibacy. She implored me to practise the ascetic brahmacharya of my ancestors (p. 15).

Madeleine adopts Buddhism as a way to escape from personal failure as well as frustration born out of her maladjustment with religious principles. In her attempt to provoke Rama to "practise the ascetic brahmacharya", she disapproves the Feminine Principle. Ramaswamy described her way of living life:

> I often heard her in the night, saying some mantra or doing japa, and I wondered where she had gathered so much ritualistic

> wisdom. She spoke with greater and greater authority on Buddhism. Her insight into Buddhism was more psychic than religious. She read Sri Aurobindo, too, and found a great deal to approve of in the philosophy of this great philosopher and saint. 'This is what the world needs', she said once, "but I, prefer mysteries and things ancient. I shall stick to my bonzes," she concluded, laughing". (p. 312).

For Madeleine, in the words of C.D. Narasimhaiah,

> Spirituality consisted in mortification of the flesh while what needed to be mortified, transcended that is, was the self in her so as to pave the way for the self to lose its identity and rejoice in the knowledge of the Absolute[19].

In her failure as a wife and by her conversion to Buddhism, Madeleine helps Ramaswamy realize the Ultimate Truth that two spiritual and mental minds cannot meet. It also establishes the conflict of East and West Encounter.

There are numerous references of the *Ramayana* in the novel. The myth of Rama's fight to win back Sita from the clutches of Ravana is again presented from a religious point of view. Rama's victory over Ravana is mainly a victory of good over evil, and the exile of Sita is also considered as a moral demand to wage a war of 'dharma yudha' of Rama that "the dharma of a king demanded it." (p. 184). In many respects, Rama of the novel has similarity with the mythical Rama of the *Ramayana*, who is considered as the seventh Avatar (incarnation) of Lord Vishnu. If Rama of the legend is portrayed with bow and arrow, Rama of the novel is "Sagittarian by birth." (p. 19) It is significant that Rama in the novel is regarded by both the French and the Indians as kingly, almost a godly figure.

It is noteworthy to quote Bhavabhuti's *Uttara Rama Charita* regarding the relationship of Ramaswamy and Madeleine with an elemental quality which provides a universal dimension. Rama's marriage to Sita is a failure on the ground of worldly value-considerations like the marriage between Rama and Madeleine on the ideological and metaphysical ground in the novel. There are moments of bliss and happiness in their relationships but, eventually, Ramaswamy and Madeleine fall apart like the mythical hero and heroine, Rama and Sita. The *Uttara Rama Charita* discusses the pattern of life and when Rama chants the verses of Bhavabhuti, it conveys to Madeleine, which she fails to follow in the beginning, but at the end of the recitation, Madeleine understands him better. Thus it is revealed in the novel that all human sufferings are experiential and identical.

The myth of Gautam Buddha is also contextualized in *The Serpent and the Rope*. Ramaswamy is the modern version of Siddhartha. He renounces the world and sets out his journey in search of truth and makes it a quest for self-realization like Gautam Buddha. In this connection it is befitting to quote R.S. Singh who writes, "*The Serpent and the Rope* is a spiritual quest of a Jeeva for truth."[20] The hurrying hooves of Siddhartha's Kanthaka often haunt the sub-conscious mind of Ramaswamy. While convalescing in Bangalore, Rama reflects how "Kapilvastu is the true home of mankind; each one of us has Kanthaka at his door." (p. 287) This is how that Ramaswamy like a modern Buddha leaves India for a long spiritual voyage. In the beginning, he craves for worldly ideas and as a result, he falls in love with Madeleine, marries her and hopes to settle down to the comfortable life of a Professor in an Indian University. But he becomes metaphysical when the anguished cry of Savithri reaches him through her letter for spiritual unification of love in him:

> Tell me Rama, tell me truly and as before God, 'come' and I'll come. The night is so auspicious, and tomorrow is Gokulashthami, when Lord Krishna will be born. We shall fast, and we shall worship, and I shall think of you, my Lord … No Hindu woman would wed a Turk. I feel besieged – the turk is at the door. Help me to jump into the pyre. (p. 292).

Rama replies and aspires for the spiritual wedding of 'selfhood':

> Of course, there was a charger waiting for me. It would not take me to the Turk. Its name would be Kanthaka and I would change my royal garments by the Ganges, admonish

> him to return and let the people of Kapilvastu know that he, Kanthaka, was a noble steed that had led Gautama the Sakyan to the banks of the Ganges, and thus started him on the pilgrimage from which there is no returning. (p. 292).

Ramaswamy fails to make himself compatible with the idea of Savithri's marriage to Pratap. During his visit to India, Rama stays in Bombay, and, in utter despair, plunges into "the plump arms of sex-starved Lakshmi.' (p. 200). But soon he experiences that he has taken a wrong turning which reminds him of Buddha's story and his evil doings. He says, "I booked my seat on the plane somewhat secretly." (p. 296) The discovery of Madeleine in Buddhistic ascetic practices helps him in achieving the spiritual goal. As a result, he takes a divorce from Madeleine and gets him disconnected of his worldly relationship with her. He hears the call of his Guru, the Abode, the Truth, and forgets all his sufferings and regards it all as a *Maya* or a mere illusion. He decides to move to Travancore as a seeker of the metaphysical truth – the truth behind birth and death, the truth of man and that of discovering his God ahead:

> I have no Benares now, no Ganga, no Jumna; Travancore is my country, Travancore my name. Lord accept me vouch that I be where I should ... Truth indeed is He, the Guru. No, He is beyond definition. He is, and you are not. (p. 405).

Thus the myth of Gautama Buddha used here in the novel has rich symbolic implications.

Apart from it, there are also the other myths of Shiva, Parvati, Nandi, the Bull and various other allusions of Christian myths. The Yagnavalkaya – Maitreyi dialogue in the *Brihadaranyaka Upanishad* also forms a refrain in the novel. The final reference to Yagnavalkya – Maitreyi is made at the end of the novel where it indicates that it is only through a Guru and in a true spirit of humility that the true self can only be realised. It is evident in the following dialogue between Ramaswamy and Catherine which reveals the mythic connotations:

> ... That was where the Buddha had turned the wheel of Law.
>
> "No, let us go to Travancore", I said.

"Now, what is this new place?" protested Catherine.

"I have been telling you and myself a lie, all these years. My real home is in Travancore. Benares is there, and there you have no crocodiles nor pyres." ...

"I will make chocolate for two in Travancore. Travancore, Travancore, there's magic in that name!" said Catherine (p. 406).

Thus, the novel, in the view of S. Ramaswamy is "an attempt to portray the struggle of the individual to realize what he is – the self.[21]"

The myth of Shiva and Parvati is discussed in the novel in order to establish the Ramaswamy – Madeleine, and Ramaswamy - Savithri relationships. Ramaswamy and Savithri shed their worldly 'self' and come together as a mark of spiritual self like Shiva and Parvati who were a union of Absolute with the Absolute. After building the inner self, Ramaswamy feels satisfied, "And now I must find a statue of Shiva, a linga". (p. 54). Initially, Ramaswamy's love for Madeleine was a kind of worship in which one can become 'oneself' by becoming 'the other'. When Rama shows Madeleiene the huge flat stone that lay like a squat Nandi at the edge of his garden, Madeleine remarks:

> True, how very like a bull he is. You thought of Shiva, and so here is Nandi ... And she plucked some grass and gave it to him, saying. 'Now, Bull, eat! (p. 55).

Since the moment, Madeleine comes to know about Ramaswamy's God, Nandi – Lord Shiva's beloved bull at her door - and the Shiva Linga, she "never passes by the door of the garden without either touching the huge lump of the bull or caressing him." (p. 55). She even pours water on the Shiva linga.

In the words of Narsingh Srivastava, "This is the first stage of spiritual transformation that takes place in Madeleine on account of her dedication to Rama"[22].

Nandi, the vehicle of Shiva, is a manifestation of the divine self on the animal plane. And sometimes the bull "gives Madeleine happy news, for example, that she would have a son – that was about Pierre". (p. 239). Similarly, Ramaswamy and Madeleine have their elephant, and they enjoy riding on the hill. Rama and Madeleine adore Nandi at the door and elephant elsewhere with a sense of respect.

In delineating the relationship between the Indian and the Christian myths, one can witness the parallel between the begging bowl of Lord Buddha and that of the Holy Grail of Christ which is projected in the novel. The novel is full of Hindu rites and rituals like the rakhi ritual in the novel that Ramaswamy declares as a mark of brother's love to his sister and in a way, it is a quest and a love for womanhood:

> You feel the responsibility of a brother to every woman on this earth, whosoever she may be and in whatever part of the world left to himself, the Indian would have rakhi tied by every woman he met, feel her elder brother protected her love. (p. 155).

The legend of Rani Padmavathi's tying "a silken thread with Gold on it, to Emperor Akbar" (p. 156) is narrated by Ramaswamy in the novel. Rama searches for some rakhi in his room that Saroja had given to him (p. 156). Kumkum, which is considered very auspicious, is a symbol of spiritual union between husband and wife. Rama offers Sari, coconut, kumkum to Madeleine but she is disappointed to know that the gift is given by Saroja, and not by Rama. Ramaswamy is spiritually married to Savithri in his hotel room in London that he calls as a 'mystic marriage'. (p. 211). There are also references of rites performed by Rama after his mother's death. He goes to the burning Ghats with a lot of 'kumkum' that he pours on her. Rama is completely shaven as per Hindu tradition.

> I remember how when young on one day the monster ate the moon and the day fell into an eclipse, I used with 'tie' and 'kusha' grass to offer the manes my filial devotion. For withal I was a good Brahmin. I even knew grammar and the Brahmin Sutras, read the Upanishads at the age of four, was given the holy thread at seven – because my mother was dead and I had to perform her funeral

ceremonies, year after year, my father having married again. So with wet cloth and an empty stomach, with devotion, and sandal paste on my forehead, I fell before the rice-balls of my mother and I sobbed. (pp. 56).

There are countless legends and episodes which have been incorporated for evoking moral in the novel. Ramaswamy's scholarly mind traces links between various cultural influences not only from myths and legends of his Indian background but also from different cultures of the world. The resource material of a vast magnitude has been used in *The Serpent and the Rope* which aims at making the novel unified, patterned and organized in a varied manner. The mythical technique has been used, and different myths have been linked up with one another for connecting the contemporary situations. Thus the Indian myth of Radha-Krishna is linked up with the Tristian-Iseult myth, and both of them are related with Rama-Madeleine and Rama-Savithri story. The learned hero establishes the parallels between legends and co-relates the past with the present, and stresses the essential unity in oneness of all. The concrete becomes the real; 'Maya' becomes Serpent and Rope becomes reality which are essentially spiritual. Realization of this 'reality' or 'self knowledge' becomes the central theme of the novel which is expressed and illustrated in various ways through different characters.

As a matter of fact, *The Serpent and the Rope* is basically an Indian mythical novel in the great tradition of Indian epics and the Indian *Puranas*. Its plot is episodic and digressional. It is important to cite the myth of 'Budumekaye'. According to this myth, 'a young prince, exiled through the machinations of his step-mother, follows a rolling pumpkin through a forest. The pumpkin clashes against a rock, and outcomes a beautiful princess who leads the young prince to his glorious destiny which is to be the king'. It is a myth of action which is a symbol of life. It is significant that Ramaswamy remembers this story when he is going to meet Savithri after coming from India to France for the first time. Rama's rolling pumpkin leads him to fulfil his destiny and aspires to be the King of a spiritual empire.

In the novel the theme of East-West encounter also plays a vital role in the novel. One can find that in the marriage of Rama and Madeleine, there emerges the conflict of two contrary world-views, two world cultures and two contrary epistemologies which came together in the novel that finally leads to divorce. Inspite of their sharply differentiated attitudes towards life, Ramaswamy and Madeleine – the central figures – have one striking similarity as characters. They are intensely self-conscious about the epistemologies they represent. They hardly regard themselves as simple human beings. They are constantly interpreting their own actions in the light of their national and cultural commitments which remind us that East is East and West is West and the twain cannot meet.

The novel is the spiritual autobiography of the hero-narrator Ramaswamy as well as of the novelist himself. It is the rare skill and craftsmanship of the novelist that various myths and legends and rituals have been incorporated and unified in the structure of the novel. Ramaswamy is an erudite 'Brahmin' (p. 5) who is at once a contemporary and mythical figure. The various myths employed in the novel highlight the spiritual oneness between Ramaswamy and Savithri and through them Raja Rao depicts the richness of our cultural heritage. The myths of Radha, Sita and Savithri construct the sensitive mind of Ramaswamy who accentuates the glorification of the Feminine Principle in the novel where a woman becomes a mother as a symbol of creation and suffering and that of 'Mother Shakti'.

By utilizing various myths as a creative mode and by perceiving parallels between the contemporary and the antiquity, Raja Rao has successfully captivated and conveyed the theme of metaphysical quest for self-discovery and self-transformation in *The Serpent and the Rope* C.D. Narasimhaiah has rightly interpreted:

> Mr. Raja Rao has demonstrated in very convincing terms, in terms of fiction, that human relationships, no less than man's union with the Absolute, are the result not of bridges on rivers or bridge parties but the temporary suspension over 'gurgling space' and 'alone with silence'. Ironically, these temporary suspensions are the only permanent bridges that

man can build – the enactment of its truth is the contribution of Raja Rao to Fiction.[23]

It is justified to regard Raja Rao as a novelist of sacred metaphysical and mythical tradition. His works comprise layers of religion, ritual, metaphysics, myth, legend, and folklore. The Indian Vedantic vision and the wisdom of age-old scriptures – the *Vedas*, the *Upanishads* and the *Gita* are woven into the very fabric of Rao's novels. Both *Kanthapura* and *The Serpent and the Rope* integrate historical action and spiritual consciousness which make the life like projection of national and metaphysical history of the Indian life itself and Raja Rao appears as a master artist of myth-making tradition.

Raja Rao, as a traditional Indian novelist, perceives Indian Vedic tradition in the context of Indian myths and legends. His quest for the Ultimate Truth transformed the marriage of Ramaswamy and Madeleine into the metaphysical failure on the basis of their individual considerations of marriage and that of the roles of man and woman relationship. He finds the west as romantic, materialistic, physical as well as historical whereas East is classical, traditional, metaphysical and mythical in the treatment of the woman being emotionally true who inherits the world. Therefore, true woman for Rama is the Indian Savithri who possesses the virtues of mythological Savithri, Radha and Sita whom he adores.

As a typical Indian philosopher Raja Rao's aim in *The Serpent and the Rope* is to suggest that non-dualistic philosophy is the Ultimate Truth, which Indian Vedic tradition has evolved in its quest for truth. His depiction of woman as creative principle reflects his deep attachment with Indian ethos and sensibility. *The Serpent and the Rope*, in brief, mirrors Raja Rao's meticulous learning as well as his command over a number of literatures, mythologies, philosophies and religions of the world. His insight, therefore, is universal and metaphorical by implication.

On the basis of the above discussion, it is evident that Raja Rao is a myth-making novelist of traditional and spiritual motifs who communicates the conventional and traditional into the metaphysical new meaning- segments that structure our consciousness.

The *Ramayana*, The *Mahabharata* and the *Puranas* are the rich eternal sources for Raja Rao who designs his thematic patterns in varied ways in order to meet his creative purpose.

He has his spiritual moorings of Indian past that he dovetailed with the mythical experiences of the immediate present. He becomes a spiritual voyager of India and his journey of myth leads him to the ocean of myths and legends that he creates into his novel through events and characters that become the monuments of myth in Indian English fiction.

REFERENCES

1 Raja Rao: "Books which have influenced Me", *The Illustrated Weekly of India* (Bombay: Feb. 10, 1963), p. 45.

2 Shiv Niranjan: "Myth as a Creative Mode: A Study of Mythical parallels in Raja Rao's Novels", *Common Wealth Quarterly*, Vol. 4, No. 13, 1980, p. 50.

3 Raja Rao: *Kanthapura* (New Delhi: Orient Paperbacks, 1971).

4 M.K. Naik: *Raja Rao* (New Delhi: Blackie and Son Publishers Pvt. Ltd., 1982), p. 65.

5 Raja Rao: "Foreword", *Kanthapura*, p. 5.

6 R. Parthsarthy: "An interview with Raja Rao", *Span* (June 1978), p. 30.

7 Raja Rao: *The Serpent and the Rope* (New Delhi: Orient Paperbacks, 1968) Subsequent references pertain to this edition of the novel and will appear in the text.

8 C.D. Narasimhaiah: "The Metaphysical Novel (The Serpent and the Rope) and its significance for our Age" in *The Eagle and The Swan* (New Delhi: Vision Books, 1999), p. 200.

9 Chitra Sankaran: *The Myth Connection: The Use of Hindu Mythology in some novels of Raja Rao and R.K Narayan* (Ahmedabad: Allied Publishers, 1993), p. 92.

10 M.K. Naik: op. cit., p. 79.

11 Meenakshi Mukherjee: *The Twice Born Fiction* (New Delhi: Arnold-Heinemann Publishers (India) Private Limited, 1974), p.1.

12 O.P. Mathur: "The Serpent Vanishes : A Study in Raja Rao's Treatment of the East-West Theme", *The Modern Indian English Novel* (New Delhi: Abhinav Publications, 1993), p. 99.

13 Harish Raizada: "Point of view, Myth and Symbolism in Raja Rao's Novels", *Perspectives of Raja Rao* ed. K.K. Sharma (Ghaziabad: Vimal Prakashan, 1980), p.199.

14 Som P. Ranchan and B.M. Razdan: "The Serpent and the Rope", *The Illustrated Weekly of India* (Bombay: April 1966) p. 33.

15 Heirich Zimmer: *Myth and Symbols in Indian Art and Civilization*, ed. Joseph Campbell (Princeton: Princeton University Press, 1974), pp. 25-26.

16 In the *Mahabharata* Savithri marries, against all odds, Satyavan (The Truthful) and conquers him back from Yama, The God of Death (p. 360).

17 Stephan Hemenway: "Raja Rao's *Kanthapura* and *The Serpent and the Rope*", *The Novel of India* (Calcutta: A Writer's Workshop Publication, 1975), p. 91.

18 D.S. Mani: "Raja Rao's Vision, Values and Aesthetics", *Perspectives on Raja Rao* ed. K.K. Sharma (Ghaziabad: Vimal Prakashan, 1980), p. 11.

19 C.D. Narasimhaiah: op. cit., p. 229.

20 R.S. Singh: "A European Brahmin : Raja Rao's", Indian Novel in English (New Delhi: Arnold Heinemann, 1977), p. 87.

21 S. Ramaswamy: "Self and Society in Raja Rao's *The Serpent and the Rope*", *Aspects of Indian writing in English*, ed. M.K. Naik (Delhi: MacMillan, 1979), p. 207.

22 Narsingh Srivastava: "Love and Divorce in *The Serpent and the Rope*", Quest No. 97, Sep. and Oct. 1975), p. 60.

23 C.D. Narasimhaiah: op. cit., p. 241.

3

The Man Eater of Malgudi: Myth as Metaphor

R.K. Narayan is a prominent Indian novelist and short-story writer in English. He is one of the 'Big Three' of Indian writing in English and Mulk Raj Anand and Raja Rao are other novelists who constitute the body of first generation of Indian Novelists in English. If Anand is a social critic, and Raja Rao a metaphysical novelist, R.K. Narayan is certainly a pure artist who used his art as an end in itself. The opening part of the Chapter traces the influences upon R.K. Narayan, and then, evolves a perspective by discussing the earlier works of Narayan in a chronological manner. The later part, of course, discusses *The Man Eater of Malgudi* in terms of metaphors operating within a mythical structure.

R.K. Narayan is known as a writer of realistic fiction which is characterized by his peculiar irony and humour. In *My Days* (1975), Narayan says that his ambition was to be "a modern story-writer, a realistic fiction writer in English"[1]. As a realistic novelist, Narayan deserves all praise and a critic, Britta Olinder, admires, "Narayan's realism is above all seen in his drawing of the background, the day to day life"[2]. Among all the Indian English novelists of the first generation, Narayan has the distinction of being a pure artist, who does not propagate his political, economic, moral or religious views like Mulk Raj Anand, a propagandist and a spokesman of the untouchables, of the poor, and the down-trodden. Narayan's art is pure and perfect like any objective artist. He projects events and characters as they appear to be not as they should be.

Narayan presents a slice of life in his works with perfect

sincerity and truthfulness. He amuses and entertains his readers by using irony and humour realistically and vividly. Objectivity and impartiality are the hallmarks of his genius. He presents both aspects of life good and evil impartially. His writings are entirely free from any ideological prejudices. He holds a mirror of society and tries to present the correct image of events and people in it without any distortions.

Narayan's realistic novels do have a mythical dimension and his sources of material in myths and legends are quite rich, but his technique is different from that of Raja Rao. He uses myths taken from tales of the *Ramayana*, the *Mahabharata* and the *Puranas*. He also projects the local legends, folklore as well as primitive rituals like the ritual for rain, for harvest or ritual for fertility of land or for a woman.

The *Ramayana*, like other epics, has been the great source of inspiration to R.K. Narayan. One can witness in the *Ramayana* the ancient and popular Indian myths which can transcend the literary significance into the devotional ethics and the ethical contexts into the philosophical meanings. Narayan writes in this connection:

> It may sound hyperbolic, but I am prepared to state that almost every individual among the five hundred millions living in India is aware of the story of the *Ramayana* in some measure or other. Every child is told the story at bedtime. *The Ramayana* pervades our cultural life in one form or another at all times. Every one knows the story but loves to listen to it again *The Ramayana* in the fullest sense of the term could be called a book of perennial philosophy[3].

R.K. Narayan has extensively used the sacred stories and myths in his novels. According to Narayan, "legends and myths as contained in the *Puranas* are mere illustration of the moral and spiritual truths"[4]. He further says "The character in the epics being essentially prototypes and moulds in which humanity is cast, they remain valid for all times"[5].

Myths offer the patterns of traditional motifs and symbols for communicating meanings. Narayan has used the mythic events and characters in the form of metaphors in order to make the sense and meaning of the story clear, impressive and appealing. According to Narayan, "Every story has implicit in it, a philosophical or moral significance, underlying the distinction between good and evil"[6]. It is the dynamism of good and evil – god and demon that seems to inspire Narayan in giving us the imaginative rendering of myths in a setting which is, at once, local, regional and universal. Harish Raizada writes,

> Though R.K. Narayan is not a didactic novelist, he has extra-ordinary power of evoking a sense of propriety in life. Though not a critic of society, he is certainly a critic of conduct. If he is read thoroughly, there emerges a definite view or vision of life from each of his works[7].

R.K. Narayan has consciously made a sustainable use of myth and folklore in his novels. The imaginative treatment of mythological incidents and situations is discernable in his novels. Myth and symbolism emerge as the significant creative mode of his technique to convey a meaningful worldview of human reality in terms of shared human experience. Further, it is true that the extent of the use of myth may differ in his various novels in different ways.

Swami and Friends[8] (1935) launched Narayan into the world of the great novelists. The novel describes the life of boys in South India schools, and much of Narayan's personal experience has gone into the making of the novel. The plot revolves round the activities of Swami, the hero and his friends Mani Shanker, the most intelligent boy of the class, Somu, the monitor, Samuel, the short-statured, and so called the Pea, and Rajam, the son of the Police Superintendent. The novel is remarkable for the author's understanding of child psychology and for depiction of the carefree, buoyant world of school-days in the most realistic and convincing manner. It mirrors the life of teachers and students. There is obviously no mythical dimension in the novel. But the creation of the fictional Malgudi as a typical South Indian town in it is a new myth which is created by the novelist himself. In the novel, the incident of launching a paper-boat with an ant-seated in it in a flowing gutter is narrated as the folk-key on the basis of the Indian folklore.

The *Dark Room*[9] (1938) is a moving tale of a tormented wife. Ramani, the office secretary of Engladia Insurance Company, is very domineering and cynical in his ways and governs his house according to his own sweet will. As he is always irritable, the atmosphere of his house is generally gloomy and his wife, children and servants always remain in a state of terror. His wife Savitri is a true symbol of traditional Indian womanhood. She is very beautiful and deeply devoted to her husband. Ramani, however, does not respond and regard her sentiments. Even after their marriage for fifteen years, his wife has received nothing from her husband except rebukes and abuses. She becomes a living myth of a suffering housewife in India and in the world of Malgudi.

Ramani's lustful love for a beautiful lady, Shanta Bai, upsets the peace of his domestic life. Finding no path for correcting her husband, Savithri revolts against him, flings away all her jewellery in a huff and starts living in the dark room. In the state of despair, she leaves her home and tries to commit suicide. But finally, she realizes the futility of her bonds in the temporal world and returns home. It is a story of a helpless housewife in Indian family.

The novel *The Dark Room* seems to refer to the *Ramayana*. Savitri of the novel parallels Kaikayee, one of the three wives of Dasharatha in the *Ramayana*. Kaikayee enters 'Kopbhaven' for fulfilling two boons once promised by Dasharatha to her. One boon refers to the throne for her own son, Bharata while the other boon refers to a fourteen-year banishment for her step-son, Rama. Similarly, in the novel, Savitri goes to 'the dark room', which is a parallel to the mythical 'Kopbhaven', where she discovers her husband's infidelity. *The Dark Room* appears to a realistic myth in the modern context.

The English Teacher[10] (1946) tells a love-story which is entirely different from the conventional love stories. It narrates the domestic life of Krishnan, a lecturer in English, in Albert Mission College, Malgudi. Though he is only thirty years old, he feels bored with life in the absence of his wife and baby daughter. They arrive after a few months, along with his mother. Krishnan and his wife Susila lead a happy life for several months. But their happy married life is short-lived. Susila falls ill and remains bed-ridden. Though Susila's illness is diagnosed as typhoid, the best available treatment does not cure her. Finally, she dies and it tells the autobiographical vein of the novelist himself.

It is a great shock to Krishnan. He is much upset, and loses all interest in life and in his work. The only comfort to him is his little daughter, Leela, who absorbs much of his time and attention. He frequently wanders about a lotus-pond, where he meets a Sanyasi (the hermit) who can communicate with spirits of the dead. Through him Krishnan is able to establish a psychic communication with the spirit of his dead wife. Finally, the boundaries of their personalities are dissolved and they become one.

The novel illustrates the ancient tale of Satyavan and Savitri and presents a reversal of the protagonist's role in terms of gender. It is Krishnan, but not Susila, who appears to be the protagonist. Therefore, Krishnan's role is largely elaborated in the novel. In the myth, it is Savitri who brings back the soul of Satyavan from the God of Death (Yama) but in the novel it is Krishnan who makes relentless efforts to establish a psychical contact with the spirit of his dead wife, Susila. The mythic cycle of Savitri and Saytavan seeks a reversal in context of Krishnan and Satyavan.

Mr. Sampath[11] (1949), like the other novels of R.K. Narayan, makes use of myth. Mr. Sampath, the titular figure of the story and an unscrupulous and cunning rogue, is the victim of high ambition and overconfidence without adequate corresponding abilities. He also resorted to agriculture. Srinivas, an idealist, is another character of the novel whose role is very important. His repeated reading of *Upanishads* makes him indifferent to his family life. He holds a philosophical attitude to life and the world. Coming from Talapur to Malgudi, he spends nearly week looking for someone who would print his journal *The Banner*. One day in The Bombay Anand Bhavan while taking a cup of coffee, he meets Mr. Sampath who agrees to print *The Banner*. The edition and publication of the *Banner* absorbs all his attention, and spares no time to think of his wife and his little son. When they suddenly arrive at Malgudi from the Village, his surprise knows no bounds. Srinivas neglects his domestic duties resulting in frequent domestic quarrels, which, however, are soon patched up.

The edition and publication of the *Banner* is suspended because of a strike in the press. The resourceful Mr. Sampath now decides to turn film producer, sets up 'the Sunrise Picture Studio' with Srinivas as the script-writer, his friend Somu as the financier, and a young man, Ravi as the accountant of the company. "The Burning of Kama" is the first film to be produced with Mr. Sampath acting the role of Shiva, and a beautiful actress, Shanti, that of Parvati. She is the idol of Ravi, and when he discovers that she is playing the role of Parvati, he runs on the stage, embraces her and takes her away. There is an uproar in the studio, much equipment is damaged, and so the film producing venture also comes to an end.

Ravi turns mad, and has to be sent to the police lock-up. Srinivas is disgusted, disconnects himself with the film-world, and revives the publication of the *Banner*. Mr. Sampath carries on for sometime with Shanti who then leaves him for good. Mr. Sampath himself has to leave Malgudi in order to escape the notice of his editors, Somu and others. The novel ends as Mr. Sampath bids farewell to Srinivas.

The novel *Mr. Sampath* is centred on the myth of the burning of Kama, the god of love, who is reduced to ashes by Lord Shiva's third eye. In Ravi's abduction of Shanti in the novel, Narayan used Sita-myth. Srinivas, the scenario-writer, traces the existence of Sarayu river of Malgudi of the Puranic times. The conflict between Srinivas and Sampath is a mythical and parallels between the good and the evil, the sura (God) and the asura (demon). Thus, by using two main myths of Shiva and Sita, Narayan successful integrates the mythic element in the novel which is a recurrent motif in the Hindu mythology. Srinivas, like Rama of the *Ramayana* struggles for order in society on the earth but is entrapped into difficult situations. But Srinivas restores peace in the end of the novel by experiencing the Upanishadic wisdom while he is beset by demon-like characters such as Mr. Sampath, Ravi and Somu like Rama who was beset by many demons. The river Sarayu stands as a unique blend of ancient myth and contemporary reality. In the words of Chitra Sankaran, "The novel described Srinivas's ontological quest for the values and meaning of existence and its relevance within the Hindu tradition"[12].

The Financial Expert[13] (1952) described the story of the rise and fall of Margayya, the financial expert. Margayya begins his career as a petty money-lender doing his business under a banyan tree, in front of the central co-operative Land Mortgage Bank in Malgudi. He helps the share holders of the bank to borrow money at a small interest and lends it to the needy at a higher interest. In the process he earns some money for himself. The Secretary of the bank and ArulDoss, the peon, seize from his box the loan application forms he has managed to get from the bank through its share-holders; treat him with contempt; and threaten to take action against him. He shows his horoscope to an astrologer and is assured that a good time is coming for him, if only he did *Puja* to Lakshmi, the Goddess of Weatlh. The *puja* is done for forty days, with ash from a red lotus and ghee made out of milk from a cow. Margayya goes through the puja and at the end, he hopes of prosperous career. The theme of the novel is lust for money, but Margayya is no monster of greed and wickedness. Narayan has succeeded in humanizing him and showing that despite his lust for money, he is a human being like us.

In the novel, the myths and symbolism appear as the significant creative mode of Narayan's technique to convey a meaningful world view of human reality. Various mythical motifs like lotus, milk, fire and banyan tree emerge as archetypal images and evoke deep emotional response in the mind of the reader because they resemble an image already registered in our unconscious mind. Owing to their universal appeal and timelessness, Narayan has found the mythical symbols a suitable creative mode for communicating the predicament of the financial expert, Margayya. The novel can be read as a moral fable on the illusion of get-rich-quick schemes of modern times. The novelist has used two symbols for wealth-milk and lotus – to narrate the story of the rise and fall of Margayya. According to the Indian mythology, Laskhmi is the goddess of opulence and fortune. "She is 'honey-like' (madhavi) and is said to grant 'gold', cows, horses and slaves' ... she is 'made of gold' (hiranyamavi)"[14]. Margayya feels that money is man's greatest need like air or food and he goes to horrifying lengths for its sake. Money gives him the feeling of being the part of an infinite existence. While Margayya lives in time, the priest in the novel lives "in a sort of timelessness"[15]. This makes the novel a cyclical representation of life itself. The novel captures and conveys some lastingly satisfying account of the experiences of the twentieth century financial expert.

Waiting for the Mahatma[16] (1955) narrates the love story of Sriram and Bharati against the background of the political life of India during the years which immediately preceded the independence of the country in 1947. *The Vendor of Sweets*[17] is the story of Jagan, a sweet-vendor. He is religious minded and has been considerably influenced by *the Gita.* He is also a staunch follower of Gandhi and tries to live up to the Gandhian way of life. In both the novel, Narayan diverts from the traditional myths and uses the newly created myth of Gandhi in these novels. Narayan has brilliantly woven the historical Gandhian myth into fine strands of love, politics and idealism.

In *The Painter of Signs*[18], the relationship between the main characters, Daisy and Raman, is based on the legendary relationship between King Shantanu and Goddess Ganga of the *Mahabharata.* Raman proposes to marry Daisy in the Gandharva style which is most suitable in the present context. It is Gandharva's Vivah, the type of marriage that one reads in classical literature. Daisy says to Raman, "If you want to marry me, you must leave to my plans even when I am a wife. On any day you question why or how, I will leave you". She makes it very clear to Raman with a mad glint in her eyes. Fascinated by her beauty, Raman is not to object to or modify it in any manner, "Whatever you say, I will never interfere. I won't question you, I will like the ancient king Santhanu"[19].

Both Daisy and Raman re-enact the mythical parallel of Santhanu and his wife Ganga in the novel.

The use of Bhasmasura myth in *The Man Eater of Malgudi*, Santanu – Ganga legend in *The Painter of Signs* and Siddhartha's enlightenment in *A Tiger for Malgudi*, project Narayan as a myth-making novelist. They express the Indian religious faith. Therefore, P.S. Sundaram observes Narayan's novels as "religious fables" [20]. His characters are often seen visiting temples and performing rituals. References to temples like Hanuman temple and Laxmi temple in *The Financial Expert* and the portrayal of Sanyasis in *The Dark Room* and *A Tiger for Malgudi* justify his deeply rooted faith in Hindu religion and ethos.

The present study ventures to highlight the use of myth as metaphor in *The Man Eater of Malgudi* (1961). The present novel is much closer to myth than the other novels of R.K. Narayan. In the novel, he beautifully transcends the ancient myths in terms of the twentieth century India. Here Narayan has successfully made use of myth in varied ways, both thematically and technically and has transformed India's remote past into our contemporary reality. *The Man Eater of Malgudi* is the only novel by R.K. Narayan which has a mythical structure which reveals Narayan's abiding interest and faith in the ancient values and his pride for the rich spiritual heritage of India. In this respect it is apt to quote Shyam M. Asnani when he writes:

> It is undoubtedly a vivid and significant phenomenon in Narayan's creative work for the imaginative rendering of the ancient Puranic myth with both serious parallelism and ironic contrast[21].

Narayan has used myth as metaphor in *The Man Eater of Malgudi*. Metaphor is a significant literary tool for formulating and projecting meaning and vision. It becomes a powerful weapon in the hands of the writer to enable the reader to understand feeling and idea, which he tries to express. It provides an insight to the writer handling his creative problem.

The Man Eater of Malgudi[22] is a modern version of the

ancient tale of Bhasmasura, a demon, which is taken from the *Mahabharata* that the novelist has used in the novel. He fuses the mythical and the contemporary characters and situations, which resemble those of the myths. The novelist here employs the Bhasmasura myth as a structural parallel while other myths like Rama-Ravana, Mahisasura, Gajendra Moksha have been used in a digressional way. All the events and characters of the novel appear like mythical metaphors.

According to M.K. Naik,

> *The Man Eater of Malgudi* is an impressive novel dealing with ethical issues such as the fate of evil and the question of human relationship and the precepts and practice of the entire business of living[23].

The novel is centred on the Shiva and Bhasmasura myth. Nataraj, the protagonist of the novel, is a printer of Malgudi. He lives a peaceful life with his employee, Sastri and a handful visiting friends in his press. Nataraj's disruption of his peaceful rhythmic life is caused by an aggressive intruder Vasu, a taxidermist, who comes to hunt out animals for his business from the surrounding Mempi jungle.

The smooth and congenial life of Nataraj and his friends is again disturbed when Vasu comes to live with them in a room in the upper storey of the printing press against Nataraj's will. Vasu's gigantic physique and his aggressive behaviour arouse fear in the hearts and minds of Nataraj and his friends. Vasu orders Nataraj to print five hundred visiting cards for him, the bill for which is never paid. As desired by Nataraj, Vasu narrates his past, explaining how under a rigorous training received from the 'Pahelwan', his master, he acquired an enormous strength and how ultimately he left him. Vasu's bullying talk is frightening to all around.

In the beginning, Nataraj tolerates him but he could not tolerate the robbing of wildlife of Mempi forest and that of collecting and stuffing dead animals in his room. When his neighbours complain Nataraj about the insanitary conditions caused by the taxidermist, he requests Vasu to vacate the house but he is surprised to learn that a complaint has been lodged against him in turn and Vasu himself tries to evict Nataraj by using the unlawful means.

Vasu has also great passion for women and as a lustful person, he brings Rangi, a notorious dancing woman with some other women like her, to his room, which creates stormy situations around him by Nataraj and others concerned.

Sastri, Nataraj's assistant, an orthodox Sanskrit scholar, always avoids Vasu. He serves as a chorus, foretells about Vasu's imminent doom of destruction by narrating the stories of certain demons like Bhasmasura and concludes that the evil has its own seeds of destruction.

Nataraj gets upset when he learns from Rangi that Vasu intends to shoot Kumar, a temple elephant, on the day of the festival celebration. He immediately gets his friends acquainted with Vasu's wicked intentions and reports the matter to the police. But they express their helplessness to take any action against Vasu until the crime has been actually committed.

Nataraj goes to his office the next morning where he comes to know that Vasu is dead. The police starts investigation in which Nataraj, his friends and Rangi, the temple dancer, are suspected about Vasu's murder. From the medical report, it is evident that Vasu died of concussion received on his right temple from a blunt instrument. When the police fail to find any clue of the culprit, the matter is dropped. Rangi, later on, tells that while striking a mosquito settled on his forehead, Vasu slapped himself and thus dies of a blow from his own hammer-fist.

The story of the novel is parallel to the Bhasmasura myth. Sastri narrates the story of Bhasmasura as under:

> There was Bhasmasura, who acquired a special boon that everything he touched should be scorched, while nothing could ever destroy him. He made humanity suffer. God Vishnu appeared as a dancer of great beauty, named Mohini, with whom the asura became infatuated. She promised to yield to him only if he imitated all the gesture and movements of her own dancing. At one point in the dance, Mohini

> placed her palms on her head, and the demon followed this gesture in complete forgetfulness and was reduced to ashes that very second, the blighting touch becoming active on his own head. Everyman can think that he is great and will live forever, but no one can guess from which quarter his doom will come[24].

In the novel, Narayan introduces the 'demon' Vasu like Bhasmasura. K.R. Srinivas Iyengar rightly comments on the demon – like Vasu who "is the killer of animals, the purveyor of carcasses the enemy of Kumar, the temple elephant and the terror of men (the 'other'), he is of blackness all compact, he glows with evil, he is the prince of darkness" [25]

Like Bhasmasura, Vasu's appearance in Malgudi is "equally sudden"[26]. As Bhasmasura comes forward as a true devotee of Lord Shiva and offers himself to the service of his creator, similarly, Vasu appears in Malgudi as a multifaceted personality- an M.A. in History, Economics and Literature, a freedom fighter, a strong man, trained under a Pahelwan as well as a taxidermist. Vasu emerges suddenly "practically tearing aside the curtain", violating "the sacred traditions" of Nataraj's press (p. 15). His appearance of Vasu in Malgudi, as he himself tells Nataraj, is on a professionl ground. "I'm here because of Mempi forest and the jungles in those hills. I am a taxidermist. I have to be where wild animals live." (p. 19).

Nataraj shelters Vasu in the attic of his press though he is not related with him. Even without Natraj's consent, Vasu establishes himself in the attic, Nataraj, out of his human considerations and good nature, compromises with the situation and utters: "Why not let him stay there until he finds a house?" (p. 26).

Like Bhasmasura, Vasu creates insurmountable problems for Nataraj and his companions and as a taxidermist he kills birds and animals and stuffs them. Consequently, there spreads an intolerable foul smell which suffocates the inhabitants of the locality. Like Lord Shiva who had given the boon of indestructibility to Bhasmasura, Nataraj runs here and there in search of help against the person who had provided his attic free of charge out of his humanity.

Vasu becomes capable of splintering "a three-inch panel of seasoned teak" with his fist, snapping "chains", twisting "iron bars" and pulverizing "granite" (p. 18). Vasu's real strength is revealed later in the novel when he talks to the police inspector cynically, "If I had hit you with my hand – do you want to see what would have happened? he brings his palm flat down on the iron frame of the cot and cracks it" (p. 151). Vasu's fist has become a myth and a metaphor and a symbol of terror which is compared with the burning palm of Bhasmasura. Vasu's handshake with Nataraj is also evident of the enormity and strength of his fist. Nataraj also feels: "My entire hand disappeared into his fist." (p. 16) Vasu makes his principle clear to Sen, the journalist, that he will not hit anyone unless he is hit first. He says, "I could settle many problems with this, but I don't. If I hit you with it, it will be the end of you. But that does not mean I may not kick" (p. 27). Bhasmasura's indiscriminate killing of the innocent creatures as well as that of human beings on the earth can be compared with Vasu in the novel who is engaged in depleting the forests of Mempi with their creatures. His hunt includes wild animals of all varieties – tiger, deer, stag, hyena, python, crow, eagle etc. The heavy loss of innocent lives caused by Vasu is observed sorrowfully by Nataraj:

> He brought in more and more dead creatures; there was no space for him in his room or on the terrace. Every inch of space must have been cluttered with packing – boards and nails and skins and moulds. The narrow staircase at which I could peep from my machine, was getting filled up with his merchandise, which had now reached the last step – he had left just enough margin for himself to move up and down. (p. 73)

Apart from it, there are several instances in the novel pertaining to Vasu's atrocity. As a hunter he is only permitted to shoot duck and deer but he shoots animals of all varieties. And in a swaggering tone, in defiance of the vigilance of the forest authorities, he says, "Now they shall know what I can do." (p. 31) Nataraj's visitors always try to run away as they catch sight of Vasu as it is difficult for them to cope with his bullying talk. For Sastri, Vasu has "all the definitions of rakshasa" (p. 75) He points out the traits which make a rakshasa "a domestic creature who possessed enormous strength, strange powers, and genius but recognized no sort of restraints by man or God." (p. 75) Sastri further says,

> Every rakshasa gets swollen with his ego. He thinks he is invincible, beyond every law. But sooner or later something or other will destroy him (p. 75).

Vasu himself says, "I challenge any man to contradict me." (p. 17) Nataraj considers Vasu "the lord of the Universe" having "no use for the people's words" (p. 33). His attitude to Vasu is well expressed in the way, he responds to Vasu's behaviour:

> His nature would not let him live anyone in peace. He'd wilt if he could not find some poor man to bully. If he found some one known to him, he taunted him. If he met a stranger or a new force, he bluntly demanded, 'who is he? You have not told me his name!' No Maharaja finding a ragged commoner wandering in the halls of his durbar would have adopted a more authoritative tone in asking, 'who is this?" (p. 27) Vasu's atrocity to the animals is viewed pathetically by Nataraj: "No creature was safe, if it had the misfortune to catch his eye." (p. 53)

The mental torture that Vasu creates upon the mind of the people is essentially violent and painful. He appears as a symbol of horror and a living God of fear in Malgudi.

P.S. Sundaram thus comments:

> Violence in any form, Narayan feels, is evil, a thing to be avoided. Compromise is always preferable to confrontation, an attitude which explains Nataraj's reaction to Vasu[27].

According to myth, Bhasmasura not only commits massacre of the innocents but also indulges himself in a rebellion against Shiva, his originator and benefactor. He threatens Shiva and endeavours to destroy him. Similarly, Vasu in the novel rebels against his trainer, a Pahelwan who has made him a strong man as well as against Natraj who provided him a shelter in his home. The ungrateful Vasu described the way he treated his master:

> I knew his weak spot. I hit him there with the edge of my palm with a chopping movement ... and he fell down and squirmed on the floor. I knew he could perform no more. I left him there and walked out, and gave up the strong man's life once and for all. (pp. 18-19).

In addition to the Pahelwan (Wrestler), Nataraj also falls a victim to Vasu's ingratitude and maltreatment. When Nataraj asks Vasu to vacate the attic, the ungrateful Vasu maltreats him. Nataraj thus utters,

> Vasu had filed a complaint against me as a landlord. There were also other minor complaints; such as that I was not maintaining the house in a habitable condition, and was involving the said tenant in great loss, damage, and expense. (p. 59).

In this context, it is appropriate to quote Meenakshi Mukherjee who writes,

> the polarity between Nataraj, the meek and tolerant printer, and Vasu, the dynamic man of action, is too clear to be overlooked. Nataraj is mainly passive, things happen to him and he has little power to influence events; while Vasu is the great advocate of individual achievement.[28]

Vasu's rivalry with nature as well as with the mankind symbolizes in his operation of stuffing animals and that of his egocentric behaviour towards anyone else. The dialogue between Nataraj and Vasu, about the bird, Garuda, strikes mythical overtones which highlight essential devilish intentions of evil-hearted Vasu:

> "You have no doubt excelled in giving it the right look, but poor thing, it is dead."
>
> "Don't you see that it is Garuda?"
>
> "What if it is?"
>
> "Don't you realize that it's sacred? That it's the messenger of God Vishnu?"

"I want to try and make Vishnu use his feet now and then". (p. 53).

Vasu ruminates for awhile over Nataraj's suggestion about the sacredness of Garuda and thinks in it a business proposition:

> I can supply them stuffed eagles at about fifty rupees each. Every one can keep a sacred Garuda in the Puja and I'll guarantee that it won't fly off. (p. 53).

It shakes Vasu's conscience who wants to do service to his religious folk by satisfying his religious sentiments.

The dialogue between Vasu and Nataraj about Garuda clears the vainglorious and obdurate pride of Vasu who challenges the Absolute, and the Divine Essence which can be considered as the very force of creation.

Vasu himself embodies the disruptive force which threatens the social order. He is a modern rakshasa (demon) who has not the supernatural powers of moving anywhere at any time nor has he the power to destroy things at will like the mythical characters of the *Mahabharata* and the *Ramayana* era. But he has a jeep and a gun which provide him power to go anywhere at anytime and to kill any creature. Therefore, William Walsh rightly treats the character, 'Vasu is one in whom the will is unqualified by the past'[29].

Bhasmasura's lust for Parvati underlines his demonic nature. Similarly, in the novel, Vasu's lust for women marks his moral degeneration. Vasu considers women as a commodity to satisfy his carnal desires only. He says without any moral scruples:

> If you like a woman, have her by all means. You don't have to own a coffee estate because you like a cup of coffee now and then. (pp. 33-34).

Vasu's sexual urge is boundless while his lust has demonic touch. As a great womanizer, he encounters a variety of women at his residence for which Rangi is no exception. Nataraj is wonderstruck to observe his lustful love for women and he thus utters:

> I was mistaken in thinking that Rangi was the only woman. I had only to stand there between seven and eight in the morning, and it became a sort of game to speculate who would be descending the stairs next. Sometimes a slim girl went by, sometimes a fair one, some-times an in-between type, some-times a fuzzy-haired woman, some-morning a fashionable one who had taken the trouble to tidy herself up before coming out. (p. 86).

According to myth, Lord Vishnu transformed himself in the form of a beautiful nymph called Mohini in order to destroy Bhasmasura. When Bhasmasura was well lost in love with Mohini, she charmingly requested him to dance like her and thus tricked him to put one of his hands on his head and as per Shiva's boon he himself was reduced to ashes. In the novel, Rangi represents the myth of Mohani, an instrument of Vasu's death. Rangi dislikes Vasu's plan of shooting the elephant. Though Vasu is not killed by Rangi, she becomes instrumental in destroying him. The novelist himself calls it as "an unconscious instrument of destruction"[30]. Rangi fans and lulls him to sleep but suddenly she goes to sleep. The mosquitoes sing and sting Vasu's forehead who gets his own fatal blow while attempting to swat the mosquito. It is his own palm, once a powerful stroke and a symbol of terror to others, that brings an end to his life.

It is noteworthy to quote R.K. Narayan who says,

> The Man-Eater is a man, not a tiger, an ego-centred man for whom the objective world is non-existent – a modern rakshasa who wants to kill the elephant that belongs to the local temple[31].

The parallel between Mohini and Rangi can be drawn at two levels: first, that Mohini is a divine dancer and Rangi is a temple dancer. Secondly, the name 'Rangi' as M.K. Naik notes, "is obviously derived from 'Ranganath', one of the appellations of Vishnu."[32] Moreover, Rangi's association with the temple is also divine and her sacrificial commitment, her concern about the safety of the temple elephant, her idea of mixing some sleep producing drug with Vasu's food are some of the good humanistic traits of her personality which brings a rightful comparison between 'Rangi' and 'Mohini'.

> However, the contrast between Mohini and Rangi is replete with irony. Mohini is a divine damsel. She has a fascinating charm. On the contrary, Rangi is an "awful fleshy creature whom Sastri considered a sin to look at" (p. 119). Mohini contains the androgynic trait of Vishnu. But Rangi is "a perfect female animal" (p. 85). Mohini is an accomplished dancer while Rangi's dance, on the other hand, displays "only of a few formal flourishes of her arms," which is unimpressive and not cared by anyone (p. 122).

Like Bhasmasura, Shiva and Vishnu as Mohini, there are other myths of Ravana, Mahisasura and Gajendra Moksha which can be described as a mythic metaphor. The myth of Ravana also resembles Vasu. Sastri says,

> There was Ravana, the protagonist in the *Ramayana* who has ten heads and twenty arms, and enormous yogic and physical powers, and a boon from the gods that he could never be vanquished. The earth shook under his tyranny still he came to a sad end. (p. 76).

Like Bhasmasura, Ravana too had tried to dislodge the Lord Shiva from the Kailash Mountain which is considered as the abode of his boon-giver, Lord Shiva. In the novel, Vasu tries ro dislodge Nataraj from the respectable position, which he had in the society and also dislodges him from the printing press. Ravana's "enormous physical power" (p. 76) can find a parallel in Vasu's physical power. Bragging of his powers, Vasu claims that his aim is to prove human superiority to nature, and tells Nataraj: "Science conquers nature in a new way everyday; why not in creation also? That's my philosophy." (p. 17).

One can witness another myth of Mahisasura in the novel "who meditated and acquired a boon of immortality and invincibility, and who had secured an especial favour that every drop of bloodshed from his body should give rise to another demon in his own image and strength, and who nevertheless was destroyed. The Goddess with six arms, each bearing a difficult weapon, came riding for the flight on a lion which sucked every drop of blood drawn from the demon." (p. 76).

In Vasu's case, his powerful fist represents an illusion of invincibility which ultimately becomes an instrument of his death. Nataraj refers to the myth of Daksha, "for whom an end was prophesied through the bite of a snake, and he had built himself an island fortress to evade his fate, and yet in the end he died." (p. 76).

The novelist also discusses the myth of Gajendra Moksha. After Vasu's decision to shoot the temple elephant, Kumar, reminds Nataraj of "the tale of elephant Gajendra, the elephant of mythology who stepped into a lake and had his leg caught in the jaws of a mighty crocodile; and the elephant trumpeted helplessly, struggled, and in the end desperately called out Vishnu, who immediately appeared and gave him the strength to come ashore out of the ways of the crocodile." (p. 139).

Nataraj believes in the power of Lord Vishnu and feels that just as Lord Krishna saved the life of Gajendra, the mythic elephant, similarly Lord Krishna would save Kumar, the temple elephant, too. Meenakshi Mukherjee observes the conflict as a battle between good and evil in society:

> The conflict is not between Vasu and Nataraj alone but between Vasu and society in general, and Vasu's seeming superiority over so vast a force merely underlines the fact that evil is often far more dynamic than the forces of goodness"[33].

Nataraj's liking for Vasu in the beginning of the novel shows that evil is not only stronger but is also more attractive than goodness. In the words of Nagendra Nath Sharan,

The novel acquires the suspense of a detective novel when Vasu, the embodiment of evil, meets his mysterious end. Irony reaches the pitch of its powers. It becomes an instrument of moral discovery. Narayan succeeds in grafting a modern narrative based on the ancient Indian myth[34].

The novelist utilizes the possibilities of the age-old Indian myths in *The Man Eater of Malgudi* and, according to a critic, "transcends the narrow political, social, and cultural frontiers and embraces human values that are valid for all times and climes."[35] His use of Bhasmasura myth and other myths like Rama-Ravana, Mahisasura, Daksha and Gajendra Moksha in *The Man Eater of Malgudi* bring forth a conscious literary technique. Here the pace of narrative is faster than what we have seen in his other novels – *Swami and Friends*, *The Dark Room*, *The English Teacher*, *Mr. Sampath*, *The Financial Expert*, *Waiting for the Mahatma* and *The Painter of Signs*. It seems that a demon like Vasu has set his own mythic pace in the novel.

The Man Eater of Malgudi has a rich and highly integrated mythical structure. Many similarities with the *Puranas* in the novel carry out Narayan's art which highlights the moral values prevailing in the society as well as in the texture of the novel. In this relation it is apt to mention Rajesh K. Pallan who rightly summarizes that 'an essential pattern in Narayan's *The Man Eater of Malgudi* points out Order, Dislocation of Order and Restoration of Order in society. This order is cyclic. Before Vasu's arrival on the scene, there exists the rule of order in the novel which is violently upset by Vasu's interference with the privacy of the blue curtain in Nataraj's room. At the end of the novel, Order is again restored and the blue curtain of the printer's room is peacefully drawn again. The novel ends wherefrom it had begun and thus restoring peace and harmony of the cosmos. The classical emphasis on order and harmony is related to the humanistic concerns and values. Such a balance between order and disorder, nature and reason, humanistic belief and social forces are significantly relevant to the Indian traditions which are the hallmarks of the world of R.K. Narayan.'[36]

Thus in *The Man Eater of Malgudi*, R.K. Narayan has envisaged the realm of ancient myths in the present face of society with an experience to connect contemporary reality clearly. The juxtaposing of the ancient and the modern emphasizes how an ancient fable can be contextualized to our own age. Here, the novelist champions the cause of good and ironically displays that an evil ends into misery and trouble. He emphasizes that man is the maker of himself and is accountable for his own destiny. In this connection it is pertinent to quote the novelist himself in the following dialogue which occurs in 'God and Atheist':

> An interesting exchange. To the atheist's question "Oh, come on, what about catastrophes, calamities and holocausts one sees around".

God's answer:

Most of it is man-made, and the others are caused by – we need not go into all that now. Normally the universe is stable, stars run their course without bumping into each other ... only human beings are unpredictable. They are ready to pounce on and exterminate each other individually or as groups, communities ... In all creations, human beings alone display as much ego, aggression and greed. On the other hand, animals, birds and other creatures naturally practice a philosophy of 'live and let live'. Even beasts which kill for food attack only when they are hungry. But man will attack, pillage and grab and jealously hold on it, whether it be food, money or territory.[37]

Thus, R.K. Narayana's use of myth is ironic and corrective in measure which brings the drama of good and evil, past and present in order to control man in society. His time and space are cyclic like T.S. Eliot's concept of time and history which correlates the pastness of present with the presentness of the past and that Eliot refers in *Four Quartets*.

> Time Present and time past.
>
> Are both perhaps contained in time future
>
> And time future contained in time past[38].

In brief, R.K. Narayan's adventure of myth in the *The Man Eater of Malgudi* is innovative, corrective and thought-provoking with a difference.

REFERENCES

1 R.K. Narayan: *My Days* (London : Chatts and Windus, 1975), p.102.

2 Britta Olinder: "Reality and Myth in R.K. Narayan's Novels", *The Literary Criterion*, 20, No. 2 (1985), pp. 8-10.

3 R.K. Narayan: *The Ramayana* (New Delhi: Vision Book Pvt. Ltd., 1987), p.6.

4 R.K. Narayan: *Gods, Demons and others* (Mysore: Indian Thought Publications, 1973), p.4.

5 *Ibid.*, p. 4.

6 *Ibid.*, p. 4.

7 Harish Raizada: *R.K. Narayan, A Critical Study of His Works* (New Delhi: Young Asian Publications, 1969), p.160.

8 R.K. Narayan: *Swami and Friends* (1935) (Mysore: Indian Thought Publications, 1971).

9 R.K. Narayan: *The Dark Room* (1938) (Mysore: Indian Thought Publications, 1972).

10 R.K. Narayan: *The English Teacher* (Mysore: Indian Thought Publications, 1996).

11 R.K. Narayan: *Mr. Sampath* (Mysore: Indian Thought Publications, 1956).

12 Chitra Sankaran: *The Myth Connection* (New Delhi: Allied Publishers, 1984), p. 139.

13 R.K. Narayan: *The Financial Expert* (1952) (Mysore: Indian Thought Publications, 1984).

14 Heinrich Zimmer: *Myth and Symbols in Indian Art and Civilization*, ed. Joseph Campbell, (Princeton: Princeton University Press, 1974), pp. 91-92.

15 R.K. Narayan: *The Financial Expert* op. cit. p. 24.

16 R.K. Narayan: *Waiting for the Mahatma* (1955) (Mysore: Indian Thought Publications, 1995).

17 R.K. Narayan: *The Vendor of Sweets* (1967) (Mysore: Indian Thought Publications, 1996).

18 R.K. Narayan: *The Painter of Signs* (1976) (Mysore: Indian Thought Publications, 1993).

19 *Ibid.*, p. 159.

20 P.S. Sundaram: "Naipaul on Narayan", *The Journal of English Studies*, 171 (1977), pp. 129-37.

21 Shyam M. Asnani: "The use of Myth in R.K. Narayan's Novels", *The Literary Endeavour*, Vol. III, Nos. 3 and 4, January – March 1982, April – June, 1982, p. 26.

22 R.K. Narayan: *The Man Eater of Malgudi* (1961) (Mysore: Indian Thought Publications, 1994). All the references to this novel are from this edition.

23 M.K. Naik: *The Ironic Vision* (New Delhi: Sterling Publishers Pvt. Ltd., 1983), pp. 73-74.

24 R.K. Narayan: *The Man Eater of Malgudi*: op. cit., p. 76.

25 K.R. Srinivas Iyengar: *Indian Writing in English* (New Delhi: Sterling Publishers Private Limited, 1985), p. 382.

26 M.K. Naik: "Theme and Form in R.K. Narayan's The Man Eater of Malgudi", *Dimension of Indian English Literature* (New Delhi: Sterling Publishers Pvt. Ltd., 1984), pp. 142-50.

27 P.S. Sundaram: "Naipaul on Narayan", op. cit., pp. 129-37.

28 Meenakshi Mukherjee: *The Twice Born Fiction* (New Delhi: Arnold – Heinemann Publishers (India) Pvt. Ltd., 1974), p. 147.

29 William Walsh: *R.K. Narayan: A Critical Appreciation* (New Delhi: Allied, 1983), p. 137.

30 M.K. Naik: "Theme and Form in R.K. Narayan's The Man Eater of Malgudi", *Dimension of Indian English Literature*, op. cit., p. 150.

31 R.K. Narayan: All Indian Radio Interview on Sept. 8, 1961 (Published in Writers Workshop Miscellany, No. 8, 1961), p. 50.

32 M.K. Naik: "Theme and Form in R.K. Narayan's The Man Eater of Malgudi", *Dimensions of Indian English Literature*, op. cit., p. 145.

33 Meenakshi Mukherjee: *The Twice Born Fiction*, op. cit., pp. 147-48.

34 Nagendra Nath Sharan: *A critical study of The Novels of R.K. Narayan* (New Delhi: Classical Publishing Company, 1993), p. 25.

35 Shyam M. Asnani: "The Use of Myth in R.K. Narayan's Novels", *The Literary Endeavour*, Vol. III, Nos. 3 & 4, April – June, 1982, p.30.

36 Rajesh K. Pallan: *Myths and Symbols in Raja Rao and R.K.Narayan.* (Jalandhar:ABS, Publications, 1994). p. 154.

37 R.K. Narayan: "God and the Atheist", *A writer's Nightmare* (New Delhi: Penguin, 1987), pp. 164-165.

38 T.S. Eliot: *Four Quartets*, Burnt Norton, 1-3 (Delhi: Oxford University Press, 1974).

4

Midnight's Children: Mythic Labyrinth

Salman Rushdie is one of the most powerful post-modern Indian novelists in English. He has shown a comprehensive view of novel writing by drawing the true images of the myriad aspects and problems of contemporary life in his fiction. His aim is to explore contemporary reality by using myths abundantly in his novels. History gives a limited view of reality while myths can telescope the reality. Mythic time and space may transcend the boundaries of history and it helps Rushdie in understanding the inherent elements and forces of the Universe which are operating eternally. He focuses the present and the past against the background of the universal and the eternal which makes his characters and events archetypal and imaginary in his fiction. His encyclopedic use of myths explores the deep reality behind his thematic as well as structural pattern of the novel. His contemporary history becomes a mythical history or a future history. To him, India is a disturbed and fragmented country which is reflected through his novel. It is appropriate to quote A.S. Rao who writes, "Rushdie has a knack of combining cognitive facts of life with the normative abstractions of history in his own mock serious style. He has a technique of implication with which he makes the past, present and future to bunch off at once into simultaneity of impression."[1]

Rushdie's fiction contains several Oriental and Occidental myths such as Hindu, Islamic, Greek and Christian. In *Grimus*, Persian, Greek and Norse myths are explicitly used. *Midnight's Children* contains Hindu, Greek, Islamic, Sufi and Christian Myths.

Shame deals with Greek and Norse myths whereas *The Ground Beneath Her Feet* describes Greek Orpheus and Eurydice myths. Rushdie's first fictional work *Grimus* has a distinct mythical framework which has given him a universal recognition as a great novelist of post-Independent India. The novel is a combination of myth, fantasy and science fiction where Rushdie's aim is not to depict contemporary society but to raise fundamental issues of society such as primitivism and amalgamation of various cultures in a society. The novelist's social and cultural vision in the novel has constituted the totalitarian elements of society and that of people's discontentment and revolt against it. The novel is a kind of struggle of the 'good' which is represented by Flapping Eagle against the evil that is represented by Grimus. The novel contains the Persian myth of Simurg, Greek myths of Phoenix, Hercules, Atlas, Sisyphus, Prometheus, and the Norse myth of Yggdrasil. Among these myths the myth of Simurg plays a vital role in the novel. The novelist craves for a good and humane society for the betterment of humanity on the earth.

In *Shame*, Rushdie portrays the psychological crisis of the uprooted mass of partition. The content of the novel is contemporary history of Pakistan after 1947 in which the novelist satirizes the rule of dictator in Pakistan. The novel is a story of shame of the people of Pakistan and that of suppression of shame which generates violence and communalism as faced by three families - the Shakils, the Harappas and the Hyders. The novel is also a political allegory and the major characters involved in politics represent actual political figures of Pakistan. There are two main characters in *Shame* – Omar Khayyam, Shakil and Sufiya Zenobia. They represent and generate shamelessness and shame respectively. Rushdie's use of mythic perspective regarding Pakistan makes his expressions more authentic and emphatic. He has used the myth of Sufiya Zinobia who is presented as a supernatural being, which highlights Rushdie's own revolt against political trends prevailing in Pakistan. Sufiya Zinobia in the novel *Shame* represents the myth of Pandora which is complex, confusing and problematic.

In *The Ground Beneath Her Feet* he uses a mythical world of narrative about modern India which is centred in Bombay,

Mexico and U.S.A. The Greek Orpheus and Eurydice myth constitutes the mythical pattern of the story of the novel. In the novel, Ormus Cama is a modern Orpheus and his beloved Vina Apsara is a modern prototype of Eurydice. The divine love of Vina and Ormus Cama presents love as the highest spiritual realization as well as a holy passion. But, it is not different from the love of devotee for his Maker. *The Ground Beneath Her Feet* also conveys that the contemporary civilization has become too much logical, rational and mechanical. Therefore, modern life has become absurd and superfluous. The novelist realizes that intellect and rationality alone cannot solve the intricacy and complexity of contemporary life. It is only soothing music and love which can strengthen cheerfulness of human beings. The use of myth in *Grimus*, *Shame* and *The Ground Beneath Her Feet* establishes Rushdie as a myth-maker novelist.

Rushdie's *Midnight's Children* established him as a great literary figure of international repute. He has made a multipurpose use of myth which has significantly contributed and shaped the course of Indian writing in English and which won for him the Booker prize in 1993. The novel was selected as the best novel to be awarded the Booker prize after 25 years. William Walsh rightly points out that the "huge purpose" of Salman Rushdie's *Midnight's Children* is "the personification and realization of Indian life."[2] The novel is a piece of 'fiction-faction' by one born in India but settled abroad who tries to recreate his homeland by mixing memory with desire, fact with fantasy, reality with vision and time with timelessness.[3] Rushdie suggestively remarks:

> And one such suspicious generalization may be that writers in my position: exiles or emigrants or expatriates, are haunted by some sense of loss, some urge to reclaim to look back, even at the risk of being mutated into pillars of salt, but if we do look back, we must also do so in the knowledge – which gives rise to profound uncertainties – that our physical alienation from India almost inevitably means that we will not be capable of reclaiming precisely the thing that was lost; that we will, in short, create fictions, not actual cities

or villages, but invisible ones, imaginary homelands, India's mind.[4]

In *Midnight's Children*, the imaginary truth is conveyed through a complex strategy which is centred around the narrator – protagonist Saleem Sinai who is the embodiment of a supreme moment of history that crystallizes the evolving mood and distillation of nostalgic, critical and philosophical vision. In the novel, Rushdie uses the traditional oriental method of narrative. He has tried to write a new Mahabharata of human history which deals with expansive and exclusive memory and vision of the protagonist who, according to O.P. Mathur, "is able to project a sort of prismatic vision of reality, partial, fissured and fragmented but highly absorbing and deeply meaningful."[5]

In *Midnight's Children* the experiences of three generations of Sinai family are faithfully recorded. It is the only Indian English novel which deals with the entire Indian sub-continent and traces the multi-dimensional historical development from the second decade of the twentieth century up to the emergency in 1970s. The novel covers different periods of Indian history such as the era of British rule, the struggle for independence, partition, the progress of the two nations of India and Pakistan, Indo-Pakistan wars, the creation of Bangladesh and Indian politics of the 1970s.

Linda Hutcheon categorizes *Midnight's Children* as a "histriographic metafiction", i.e. "novels which are both intensely self-reflexive and yet paradoxically also lay claim to historical events and personage ...". [6] Rushdie presents the Indian sub-continent with various features through the protagonist, Salman Sinai who is born at midnight at the dawn of Independence. The protagonist Salman Sinai and the novelist Salman Rushdie are, at times, identical. The novel delineates three generations of Sinai family living in Srinagar, Agra, Bombay and Karachi. The personal story of the family of Salman Sinai mixes with the history of India at crucial junctures and the novel becomes a tale told by Saleem to Padma mixing history with fantasy.

Saleem becomes a witness as well as a participant of the global scenario which surrounds the sub-continent. He is a mere choric commentator who decides his requisite role in a historical sense of inevitability. The novelist expresses a ghastly reality as a substitute for objective reality which reflects the novelist's genius.

Saleem Sinai opens the novel by explaining that he was born on midnight, August 15, 1947 at the exact time when India gained its Independence from British rule. At his thirty-first birthday, Saleem feels that his body is cracking and he is falling apart and fears that his death is imminent. Therefore, he grows anxious to tell his life story to Padma, his loyal and loving companion, serves as his patient, who often happens to be his sceptical audience.

Saleem's story begins in Kashmir, thirty-two years before his birth, in 1915. Saleem's grandfather, a doctor named Aadam Aziz, treats a woman, Naseem, who later on becomes Saleem's grandmother. After the marriage of Aadam Aziz with Naseem, the couple moves to Agra, where Aadam Aziz as a doctor feels loss of religious faith which has affected him deeply and finds how protests in the name of independence were violently suppressed. Aadam and Naseem have three daughters, Alia, Mumtaz, and Emerald, and two sons, Mustapha and Hanif. Aadam becomes a follower of the optimistic activist Mian Abdullah, whose anti-partition stance eventually leads to his assassination. Following Abdullah's death, Aadam hides Abdullah's frightened assistant, Nadir Khan, even despite his wife's opposition. Nadir Khan falls in love with Mumtaz, and both are secretly married. Abandoned by her husband, Mumtaz agrees to marry Ahmed Sinai, a young merchant, who until then had been courting her sister, Alia.

Mumtaz changes her name to Amina and moves to Delhi with her husband. As being pregnant, she goes to a fortune-teller who delivers a cryptic prophecy about her unborn son, and declares that the boy will never be older or younger than his country and claims that he sees two heads, knees and a nose. After attack of a terrorist organization which burns down Ahmed's factory, Ahmed and Amina move to Bombay. Young Saleem has an enormous cucumber like nose and blue eyes like those of his grandfather, Aadam Aziz. His mischievous sister, nicknamed him as the Brass monkey, is born a few years later. Saleem realizes that he has the power of telepathy and can enter anyone's world of thoughts. Eventually, Saleem begins to hear the thoughts of other children born during the first hour of Independence. The 1001 Midnight's children - a number reduced to 581 by their tenth birthday – all have magical powers, which vary according to how much close to midnight they were born. Saleem discovers that Shiva, the boy with whom he was switched at birth, was born with a pair of enormous, powerful knees and a gift for combat.

One day, Saleem loses a part of his finger in an accident and is rushed to the hospital, where his parents learnt that according to Saleem's blood group, he could not possibly be their biological son. After he leaves the hospital, Saleem is sent to live with his uncle Hanif and aunt Pia for a while. Saleem returns home to his parents shortly and Hanif commits suicide. India goes to war with China, while Saleem's perpetually congested nose undergoes a medical operation. As a result, he loses his telepathic powers but, in return, gains an incredible sense of smell, with which he can detect emotions. Saleem's entire family moves to Pakistan after India's loses war against China. During the air raids, Saleem gets hit in the head by his grandfather's silver spittoon, which erases his memory entirely.

Relieved of his memory, Saleem is reduced to an animalistic state. He meets Parvati – the witch of Midnight's children, who reminds him of his name and helps him escape back to India. Disappointed that Saleem will not marry her, Parvati – the witch, has an affair with Shiva, who has become famous as a war hero. Relationship between Parvati and Shiva quickly sour, and she returns to the magician ghetto, pregnant but still unmarried.

After the birth of Parvati's son, the government destroys magician's ghetto. Parvati dies while Shiva captures Saleem and brings him to a forced sterilization camp. Saleem divulges the names of other Midnight's children there one by one and the Midnight's Chi'dren are rounded up and sterilized, effectively destroying the powers that even threaten the Prime Minister Indira Gandhi. Later, however, Indira Gandhi loses her first election that she once held.

While in Bombay, Saleem eats some Chutney which tastes exactly like that of Mary who used to make it. He finds the Chutney factory that Mary now owns where Padma works as a gate keeper. Saleem's story thus comes full circle. His historical account is finally complete and Saleem finally decides to marry Padma, his lover and listener, on his thirty-first birthday, which falls on the thirty first anniversary of India's Independence.

Saleem Sinai is thus the central consciousness as well as 'inclusive consciousness' of the novel. He is a member of hordes of midnight's children who belong to the eventful era of post-Independence. Indian historical conditions are lost in the figure of anonimity. It not only reflects the personalized agony of an individual but also expresses collective consciousness of society. Society is the worst sufferer at the hands of ruling elite and is punished for no fault of them. They are virtually dispossessed and alienated, despite all the euphoria of first phase of Independence. Rushdie gives vent to such feelings of 'national angst' or 'social angst' which is reflected through the protagonist Saleem Sinai who becomes Rushdie's mouthpiece in the novel which could be seen in the following textual quote:

> During the first hour of August 15th 1947 – between midnight and one A.M. – no less than one thousand and one children were born within the frontiers of the important state of India... what made the event noteworthy was the nature of these children, even one of whom was, through some freak biology or owing to some preternatural power of the moment or just conceivably by sheer co-incidence endowed with features, talents or faculties which can only be described as miraculous.[7]

It is through Saleem's consciousness that all events are reminiscised. Rushdie expresses them as a part of the workings of his political unconsciousness. All the major events and episodes parade in quick succession before the mind's eye of the reader. This provides enough evidence for the Panoptic Vision of the novelist. The narrator observes:

> I must commence the business of remaking my life from the

> point from which it really begins some thirty two years before anything as obvious, as present, as my clock ridden, crime stained birth. (p. 10).

Rushdie uses a masters trope of anxiety coupled with dichotomy in order to provide a critique of history and modern times. George Lukacs, commenting on such works which combine these techniques in his article, "The Ideology of Modernism", says:

> A similar attenuation of reality underlies Joyce's stream of consciousness. It is of course intensified, where the stream of consciousness is iteslef, the medium through which reality is presented.[8]

Rushdie has captured the aspirations, emotions and dilemmas of the protagonist with this technique.

The main theme of the novel is history – the history of the Indian sub-continent. Rushdie's history is a history of social and political consciousness. The novel tries to move beyond history for the purpose of finding out universal significance of the historical events working in the particular phase of time, which heightens the extensive use of myth in it. In the words of Uma Parmeswaran:

> *Midnight's Children* is an excellent novel, that it gives us a variety of ideas and techniques, that it gives a fairly authentic history of contemporary India in the matter of facts, but that its interpretation of history is not always reliable[9].

The novel uses a mythical pattern of narrative, for exploring the historical and political situations of Indian sub-continent. Rushdie has used the technique of mythical chapter headings in the novel, too, which contains chapters like "Many-Headed Monsters" and "Revelations". The chapter called "Many Headed Monsters" reminds us of the evil deeds of Ravana who was the mythical Monarch of Lanka. The novelist's myth of Hanumana is instrumental in burning down the godown of Ahmed Sinai. The chapter describes the evil aspects of partition where undesirable currents of history took the form of many-headed monsters who are none but rioters and plunderers of the peace between the Hindus and the Muslims, the Ravana gang and that of Ahmed Sinai. By using the myths of Ravana and

Hanumana, Rushdie deplores partition which brought the evils of violence and communalism in the society.

All the characters in the novel are mythically structured as they bear mythical names such as Saleem Sinai, Padma, Shiva and Parvati Layolah, which points out religious and mythical dimension as well as allegorical and symbolic implications. The name of Saleem Sinai, a typical protagonist created by Rushdie, is presented as a Prophet Muhammad whose function is to announce the end indicating the failure of the ideal of Indian Independence. The name Sinai includes a pre-Islamic myth also:

> Sinai contains Ibn Sina, master magician, Sufi adept, and also Sin the moon, the ancient god of Hadhramaut, with this own mode of connection, his powers of action at a distance upon the tides of the world.

But Sin is also the letter S, as sinuous as a snake; serpents lie coiled within the name. And there is also the accident of transliteration – Sinai, when in Roman script, though not in Nastaliq, is also the name of the place of revelation, of put-off-thy-shoes, of commandments and golden calves; but when all that is said and done; when Ibn Sina is forgotten and the moon has set; when snakes lie hidden and revelations end; it is the name of the desert – of barrenness, infertility, dust; the name of the end. (pp. 304-305).

The myth relating to the origin of Islam and the status of the prophet, and that of the imaginary facts succinctly sum up the protagonist's destiny as well as the political situation of India:

> Prophets are not always false simply because they are overtaken, and swallowed up by history. Men of worth have always rounded the desert. (p. 305).

The name of Sinai implies "Sinai, which in Roman Script is also the name of the place of revelation, of put off thy shoes, of commandments and golden calves' ... (p. 305). The reference of Sinai suggests "Mount Sinai" where the prophet Musa or Moses heard disembodied commandments ... " (p. 163) and the alternation from the appearance of Yahveh to "disembodied commandments" in fragments underlines the development of midnight children's conference. His name also implies utter fiasco of Indian political failures – "barrenness, infertility, dust; the name of end?" (p. 305). The meaning of Sinai, also indicates the shadows of sterility gradually pervading free-India.

The nature and action of characters with mythical names like Saleem, in a prophetic and godly role: Shiva with his destructive and procreative roles; Padma's role as a nurse in a protective role of Saleem and Parvati Layolah help Rushdie to construct a mythical dimension in the novel which reflects the contemporary Indian reality. Padma, Saleem's loving companion and caretaker, becomes his fiancée at the end of the novel. She is also the audience for Saleem's narrative. With strong, hairy forearms, a name associated with dung, and a cynical and often impatient ear, Padma represents as the antithesis of Saleem's magical, exuberant, freewheeling narration. In a rhetorical device, Padma becomes instrumental for Rushdie to acknowledge the doubts and frustrations of the readers which make the great response in the novel. Saleem's frequent interruptions, digressions, and self-obsession can be equated with Padma's expressions of doubt and frustration. Both create a holistic reading experience of the novel.

Padma appears in the novel in three forms – the chorus character is Padma Mahalaxmi Racecourse, where Amina Sinai wins in the horse races and is "named after the Goddess of Wealth" (p. 139); Another name is the river Ganges who is also called Padma in Bangladesh. The monkey who scatters the money of Ahmed Sinai and that of his friends is named "the Hanuman of flying Charlots". (p. 85). The gang of terrorists is considered as the Ravana gang which means the horrible mischiefs. The role of Shiva is both destructive as well as procreative and is modelled on Lord Shiva. Born at the 'stroke of midnight' Shiva resembles the Hindu god of destruction who is Saleem's rival and counterpart. Even being born with Saleem, Shiva is robbed of his affluent birthright and is projected in abject poverty. He is blessed with a pair of enormous and powerful knees and is a gifted warrior and, therefore, he stands as a foil for the more mild-mannered Saleem.

Shiva represents another face of India: poor, Hindu as well as aggressive and passive like Saleem. As a young child, he had been the leader of a street gang and possibly a murderer. The narrator thus comments:

> To be honest: I did not like Shiva. I disliked the roughness of his tongue, the crudity of his ideas; and I was beginning to suspect him of a string of terrible crimes – although I found it impossible to find any evidence in his thoughts, because he, alone of the children at midnight, could close off from me and part of his thoughts he chose to keep to himself – which, in itself, increased my growing dislike and suspicion of the rat-faced fellow. However, I was nothing if not fair; and it would not have been fair to have kept him apart from the other members of the conference ... Shiva's conviction that he (or he and I) was the natural leader of our group by dint of his (and my) birth on the stroke of midnight had, I was bound to admit, one strong argument in its favour. It seemed to me then – it seems to me now – that the midnight miracle had indeed been remarkably hierarchical in nature, that the children's abilities declined dramatically on the basis of the distance of their time of birth from midnight; but even this was a point of view which was hotly contested ... in the face of such a storm of protest, even Shiva changed his tune; but he was to find a new one, which would be much more dangerous – dangerous for the children and for me. (pp. 226-227).

Although he is a violent character, nonetheless, he is also a tragic figure, damaged and shaped by the forces of history and class. During the 1971 war between India and Pakistan, Shiva earns name and becomes a war hero and promoted to the rank of Major. Apart from his military reputation, Shiva also becomes a noted lover among the women of Indian high society, siring a number of illegitimate children. In the end, Shiva hunts Saleem down and turns him over to one of the camps opened during Indira Gandhi's state of emergency, where Saleem, along with other *Midnight's Children*, is administered an operation that renders him sterile. In this way, Shiva manages to destroy the midnight's children effectively.

Lord Shiva is known for his benevolence, benediction and empathy for the downtrodden and the poor. In the novel, however, the character who is named Shiva serves as an anti-model to Lord Shiva even though he imbibes some of the better qualities of Lord as well. Therefore, Shiva of *Midnight's Children* who is "the most ferocious and powerful of children" (p. 282) changes the course of Indian political and social history and has a unique gift of war "of Rama, who could draw the undrawable bow; of Arjuna and Bhima, ... of Kurus and Pandavas ..." (p. 200) Shiva's victory over Saleem is a symbol of the destructive elements in Indian politics and society which prevailed during Post-Independent India.

Rushdie skilfully exploits the popular sentiments in vogue in Hindu society and offers it a novel twist and cultivates the desired Post-Modern effect. Shiva, the destroyer of midnight's children, is also a creator of future history in India for which 'Shiva-lingam' becomes mythical and symbolical:

> ... the function of Shiva-lingam, of Shiva – the procreator, so that at this very moment, in the boudoirs and hovels of the nation, a new generation of children, begotten by midnight's darkest child, was being raised towards the future (p. 441).

Because of the onwards march of history, societies cannot understand the hieroglyphic language. Symbols have lost their values and intent, especially for the highly artificial society which calls itself modern and elite. Rushdie's use therefore, of Shivalingam is in a low mimetic sense, serving as it does the disintegrating ends of societies which invite the operation of irony and satire. The character of Shiva represents such class of degenerated values of social life. His character is conceived as a 'notorious seducer', 'a ladies man', 'a cuckolder of the rich' in short a stud', (p. 408) etc.

The mythical mode is mobilised in 'fragmentation' and 'condensation' through which the novelist is successful in reaping rich dividends for the desired meanings. As Nagesh Chaturvedi while tracing myth in the novel, puts up:

Eventually the novel derives a mythical framework of narrative which helps the novelist bring out the deeper relevance of the historical political situation obtaining in the Indian subcontinent.[10]

The mythical features found in *Midnight's Children* are varied. They range from the immediate to the everlasting or eternal. Rushdie lends a deep layered significance to the characters so drawn from ancient myths and lends them social relevance with a political touch. His characters stand as the myth-makers in the novel. Padma is referred as the 'Dung Goddess', as 'Mahalaxmi' and 'Goddess of Wealth' etc. (p. 139) The myth of Shiva stands for the polluted atmosphere and stands as a keeper of social ethics and political morality in the contemporary Indian society.

Parvati, the-witch, becomes Parvathi Layolah after her marriage with Saleem Sinai. She symbolizes the secular values and that of Hindu-Muslim Unity in a religion conscious and caste conscious country like India. Thus the conglomeration of different myths creates a complex pattern by using the concept of 'condensation' and 'fragmentation' which according to John J. White, "the concept of condensation is a pattern where a number of separate pre-figurations, all related to the modern event of a single character come together."[11]

Rushdie has skilfully used 'fragmentation' as a device in the novel and by doing so he presents the myths of Ravana, Ganesh and Diana. The myth of Ganesh has been used for more than two characters in the novel, and is seen against the background of Post-Independent India. The worship of Ganesh, before conducting any religious ceremony, is the age old tradition which is not new to any Indian. It is strongly believed by Indians that Ganesh is a problem shooter and the elephant-headed Ganesh is also a God of wisdom who stands for many characters in the novel. Saleem Sinai is described as 'Mammoth Trunked', 'Ganesh nosed' elephant (p. 195). Saleem Sinai observes the state of affairs in the national political situations with the help of his nasal 'ethics' (p. 380). The ears of Ganesh are retracted across Saleem's son, Adam Sinai, who is attacked by elephants and is the real son of Shiva and Parvathi of mythical traditions. The role of 'The elephant headed

Ganesh' of the mythical past, is evident in the following lines:

He, of course, was left entirely without a say in the matter; after all, he could not even wipe his own nose at the time. He was the child of a father who has not his father; but also the child of a time which damaged reality so badly that nobody ever managed to put it together again; he was the true great – grandson of his grand father, but elephantiasis attacked him in the ears instead of the nose – because he was also the true son of Shiva – and – Parvati; he was elephant – headed Ganesh. (p. 420).

The mythical character of Ravana, the demon king of *The Ramayana,* is also mentioned in the novel. The myth of Ravana symbolizes as an evil doer and is used in a fragmented manner. He is contextual to the moral depravity in Indian politics of Independent India where the leaders of the first generation, who stood for good, left the battlefield. The situational thinking of the novelist against the back-drop of Hindu mythology of epic age becomes more comprehensible. Ravana reflects the suspicious, erratic atmosphere in the country in every walk of life. The myth of Ravana is multiple in the novel and figures as public suspicion, the Ravana gang, and that of the resultant degeneration:

> Zohra wailed in harmony with her singing breasts, 'What made people are loose in the world these days?' ... and that was how Amina heard, for the first time, the name which her husband had hidden from her, and which was, in those times, striking terror into many hearts. 'It is Ravana', said S.P. Butt ... but Ravana is the name of many headed demon; are demons, then, abroad in the land? What rubbish is this? Amina, speaking with her fathers hatred of superstition, demanded an answer; and Mr. Kemal provided it. It is the name of a dastardly crew, Madam; a band of incendiary rogues. These are troubled days, troubled days.' (p. 71).

For Muslim businessmen like Mustafa Kemal, S.P. Butt and Ahmed Sinai, public feels as "the many-headed, many-mouthed rapacious monster." (p. 71) Saleem says, "Suspicion, too, is a monster with too many heads; why, then, cannot I stop myself unleashing it at my own mother?" (p. 88)

The demonic aspect of anti-partition ethos is also concretized in the 'Ravana gang' which demands 'no partition or perdition' (p. 72). Saleem grows in such demonic atmosphere:

> Many-headed monsters swell inside me – masked Ravanas, eight-year old girls with lisps and one continuous eyebrow, mobs crying Rapist. (p. 108)

Like Ganesh and Ravana myths, the myth of Diana is also discussed in the novel. The narrator says:

> ... While Ghani the landowner stands beneath a large oil painting of Diana the Huntress, framed in squiggly gold. He wears thick dark glasses and his famous poisonous smile, and discussed art. 'I purchased it from an Englishman down cn his luck, Doctor Sahib. (p. 18)

'Diana the huntress' is a symbol of the Greek goddess of virginity and beauty, and hunting is also indicative of the change of Muslim social custom. It dramatises "perforated sheet" which is a kind of husband hunting and being enacted by Ghani, the landowner under the façade of being a lover of Muslim culture. The goddess of hunting symbolically patronizes the entanglement of Adam by Ghani and his daughter, Naseem whose illness is also a recurring affair. Dr. Aadam Aziz is "good catch for them" (p. 26), and therefore, he is frequently summoned and different parts of her body, one by one are displayed through a sheet with a hole. Aadam's observation of "wild expanses of blemished pink skin" of Diana in the portrait (p. 20) is symbolically related to his mother's reluctantly coming out of Purdah to the eyes of strangers in order to run the gemstone business only to "get pains and boils". (p. 20) It shows the impact of Western culture on Muslims through Aadam Aziz who compels his wife Naseem to give up Purdah system.

Thus the myths of Ganesh, Ravana and Diana construct a complex and fragmented pattern. Rushdie's presentation of Saleem Sinai as a narrator and Padma as a chorus character and audience embodies the narration of the novel which correlates the myth of Lord Vishnu who was narrating to Lakshmi about world drama.

Padma also enjoys a divine status in the novel as, "The lotus goddess of the present" (p. 150), "Dung goddess" (pp. 31-32) "dung flower" (p. 106) and so forth.

Rushdie has been an artist of using the myths in the form of metaphors. Shiva the character is also modelled on "Shiva, the god of destruction, who is also most potent of deities; Shiva, the greatest of dancers, who rides on a bull, whom no force can resist ... the boy Shiva had to fight for survival from his earliest days. And when his father had, about a year previously, completely lost his singing voice, Shiva had to defend himself against Wee Willie Winkie's parental zeal." (p. 221)

The mythical characters and the democratic values interact with each other in the novel. The novelist uses the myth of Brahma, a creator of the earth of different creatures and different minds and attitudes, and correlates it with the conference of Midnight's Children in Saleem Sinai's mind. The myth of Brahma also forms metaphor in the structure of the novel. Saleem says:

> Do Hindus not accept – Padma – that the world is a kind of dream; that Brahma dreamed, is dreaming the universe; that we only see dimly through that dream web, which is Maya. Maya, 'may be defined as all that is illusory; as trickery, artifice and deceit. Apparitions, phantasms, mirages, sleight-of-hand, the seeming form of things; all these are parts of Maya. If I say that certain things took place which you, lost in Brahma's dream, find hard to believe, then which of us is right?" (p. 211)

This metaphorical meanings of myth of Brahma gives an answer to the implausible and incomprehensible world created by Saleem in the novel. It is based on his dream fantasies. The novelist has selected few myths from the *Ramayana* and has used them in the form of metaphors for his ideas in the novel. The myth of Ravana stands as a metaphor of evil while the high ideas generated by Rama and Sita are metaphors which are beautifully used to face the serious question posed by the Sabaramati case.

Rushdie has used effectively the myth of Kali in the novel. He regards post-independent India as 'Kaliyuga' or 'Dark Age'.

The extensive use of Hindu myths is meant for the cause of existing evils in Indian society. The concept of Kaliyuga as an age of darkness, permeates through the guna of 'Tamas' or 'infatuation' which is the predominant characteristic. The myth of Kaliyuga is metaphorically described by the novelist for highlighting the evils prevailing in contemporary India. The evils of Kaliyuga is thus discussed in the following lines:

> Kaliyuga is the losing throw in our national dice game, the worst of everything, the age when property gives a man rank; when wealth is equated with virtue; when passion becomes the sole bond between men and women, when falsehood brings success (is it any wonder in such a time, that I too have been confused about good and evil?) (p. 194)

At the political level, the birth of Saleem Sinai announces the very birth of Independent India with partition of Pakistan on the anvil. The two become separate entities. In the case of Pakistan, it is a day earlier, as against the midnight of 14th, it is a midnight show of 13th of August in 1947. Rushdie gives vent to the feelings of 'national angst' or 'social angst' as reflected through his protagonist, Saleem Sinai. The novelist reveals through his spokesman and protagonist which could be seen in the following textual quote:

> I must commence the business of remaking my life from the point of which it really begins some thirty two years before anything as obvious, as present, as my clock ridden, crime stained birth. (p. 10)

The myth of Shakti as a simile and metaphor is also used in the context of "too much women" as a woman power (p. 406) in the novel. Saleem says:

> Too many women: are they all aspects of Devi, the goddess – who is Shakti, who slew buffalo-demon, who defeated the Orge Mahisha, who is Kali Durga Chandi Chamunda Uma Sati and Parvati ... (p. 406)

The myth of Shakti is a symbol of power in the novel. Hindu Goddesses are traditionally conceived as strong and indomitable figures. By comparing his female characters to these goddesses,

Rushdie reminds us of a woman power. He perceives India as a country of matriarchy and as an ideological country of maternal power, energy and love which is the basis of society. Through worship of the goddess mother, and women-oriented beliefs, we recognize women as the metaphor of the great power incarnate. The most remarkable symbol of the Shaktis is Shiva's spouse, who has been in variety of forms and names. The most commonplace representations are Durga, Gauri, Kali, Chandi, Parvati, Kumari and Mahadevi.

Durga is one of the most formidable and over-powering goddesses of the Hindu believers and she is also a symbol of power and grief-striker of people. Her mythological figure is to combat demons who threaten the stability of the cosmos. In this role she is depicted as a great warrior queen with several pair of arms, each wielding a weapon. She rides upon a ferocious and powerful lion and emerges as unbeatable. Durga challenges the stereotyped view of women found in traditional Hindu society. Such a characterization perhaps suggests the metaphor of super woman with extra-ordinary power which is repressed in the ordinary women who are forced into submissive and socially demeaning roles. Thus, the myth of Durga reminds us the limitless power of woman.

In *Midnight's Children*, a character named Durga dominates the scene by crushing the burly Sikh, Picture Singh, with her "preternatural breasts which unleashed a torrent of milk" (p. 448) and according to grapevine tattle, she is said to possess two wombs. Saleem acquaints us with her without really wanting to get too close to her:

> She was a woman whose biceps bulged: whose preternatural breast unleashed a torrent of milk capable of nourishing regiments; and who, it was rumoured darkly (although I suspect the rumour of being started by herself) had two wombs. She was as full of gossip and tittle-tattle as she was of milk: every day a dozen new stories gushed from her lips ... It was with the greatest reluctance that I agreed to make her acquaintance; it is with the greatest reluctance that I

admit her into these pages. (p. 445)

The novelist creates an image of Durga which also means "the unapproachable". Saleem fears her because she becomes a symbol of hope even after the consequences of the state of Emergency. Durga becomes an incarnation of the future of "new things" because "her name, even before I met her, had the smell of new things, she represented novelty, beginning the advent of new stories events complexities…" (p. 445)

She is blessed with superpower of fertility and possesses the power of foretelling even about the imminent death of Saleem, "I mention Durga the dhoban chiefly because it was she who, one evening when we were eating a meal composed of twenty seven grains of rice a piece, first foretold my death." (p. 446) According to Picture Singh, she is also responsible for the healing of Aadam Sinai, stricken with a particularly virulent case of tuberculosis. In a certain respect this imperious woman is reflected in the equally audacious, courageous Tavleen, the beautiful Canadian Sikh terrorist of flight (p. 420).

Rushdie delineates a crowd of female characters who may be compared with divine figures who can fulfil wishes and know how to predict the future. The description of these women is, however, sinister as they are mythical and unseen and the characters of Parvati and Shiva in the novel are both inspired by Hindu gods. Their stormy relationship in the novel is supposed to reflect that of the mythical gods as a positive female representation in the novel.

'Parvati' means one who dwells in the mountains as or 'the mountain girl'. Her mythology is linked with Lord Shiva's spouse. The goddess Parvati is above all known as Shiva's wife, who obtained her husband through great heroic efforts and she is the one who provokes him for creating their child in view of the conservation of the world. In *Midnight's Children* Rushdie's own version of Parvati is similar to her namesake in the novel:

> Parvati … oiled his moustache, caressed his knees and after all that produced a dinner of biriani so exquisite that he

> stopped wondering what was happening to him and began to enjoy it instead. Parvati – the-witch turned those simple Army quarters into a palace, a Kailasa fit for Shiva – the-God; and Major Shiva, lost in the haunted pools of her eyes, aroused beyond the endurance by the erotic protrusion of her lips, devoted his undivided attentions to her for four whole months; or, to be precise for one hundred and seventeen nights. (p. 411)

According to myth, Parvati gives birth to a son named Ganesh, after four months of uninterrupted coitus with Shiva. In Hindu mythology as well as in the novel, Parvati's objectives in her relationship with Shiva is the domestication of the ascetic and solitary god; in *Midnight's Children* the parallel continues in taming process which is evident in Shiva's devotion to Parvati. Parvati succeeds in subjugating Shiva who is an ascetic and erotic god of excess. Saleem informs us of General Shiva's sexual activity, "at the height of his philandering there were no less than ten thousand women in love with him." (p. 409) Parvati plays the part of moderator. As a representative housewife, she displays an ideal of controlled conjugal sexuality. However, Rushdie does not emphasize these traits in the novel. In *Midnight's Children* Parvati acts especially as a stabilizing force of restoring order. She is the one who helps Saleem return to Delhi by using her magic basket and making him invisible. She tempers even the most overwhelming Shiva's sexual urges which really was impossible before. She emerges as a positive accomplished feminine figure in the novel as carved out by the novelist.

The Prime-Minister Indira Gandhi is presented by the novelist as Goddess - Kali, Durga, Chandi, Sati and Parvati. Indira Gandhi was the Prime Minister of India from 1966-1977, then again from 1980 – 1984, a term that ended with her assassination. In her first term various political and economic reforms were made by Indira Gandhi which made her highly popular. She did an Indian Victory in the 1971 war with Pakistan and created a country of Independent Bangladesh. However, in 1971, she was found guilty of election fraud. Instead of facing charges, she declared a state of Emergency, tightening her hold over the government and ushering in a period of drastically reduced civil liberties, as well as a severe crackdown of political opposition. The emergency lasted nineteen months, after which Indira Gandhi – misjudging the extent of the population's resentment – held an open election and lost her battlefield. She stepped down but was re elected to her office in 1980. Four years later, after a disastrous series of events involving Sikh activist Indira Gandhi was assassinated by her own Sikh body-guards.

Before Indira Gandhi enters Saleem's story in a direct fashion, vague references to "the widow" hint at her eventual role in the destruction of Midnight's Children. Her actual presence in the story is brief, but of great significance. Throughout the novel, Saleem's personal life constantly reflects India's political turmoil. Finally, with the arrival of Indira Gandhi and the state of Emergency, Rushdie fuses the two narratives with a single crisis. The reforms of the emergency, which included a widespread campaign of forced sterilization, were widely seen as massive violation and abuses of government power and human rights. The nation of India is metaphorically thrown into perpetual darkness. As a result Saleem's wife, Parvati – the-witch, is killed and the famous magician's ghetto in Delhi is destroyed. By making Indira Gandhi's campaign responsible for the destruction of the fictional *Midnight's Children*, Rushdie holds her accountable for destroying the promise and the hope of a future India.

Rushdie has not only used Hindu myths but Greek myths are also effectively used in the novel. The myths of Diana, Olympus and Styx are metaphorically integrated in the novel. Olympus, the Greek mythical metaphor, is applied to Methwald's state where "Roman mansions, three storey homes of gods standing on a two storey Olympus..." (p. 94) subtly, indicates that the Britishers are ready to play their 'games' with Methwold's advocacy of colonialism and antagonistic attitude towards Indian Independence. Styx is a Greek mythical river presented as 'Stygism darkness" (p. 453) which has darkened the interior and the conscience of Indian youth. It signifies the moral decline of the country and that of the morbid future of India.

The world of Rushdie's *Midnight's Children* is a surreal

world of magic and witchery where reality is shrouded with myth and magic. It is a chaotic state of debilitation, disintegration, acrid wit animosity, distrust, corruption, debauchery, libidinousness, and torn with strifes in the life of the individuals leading to mutilations and agitations, and wars leading to massacre, rape of innocent women and killing of thousands of men and women in the name of religion or political philandering. It is not surprising if we do not find traces of ideal or romantic love in the world of *Midnight's children*.

The novel is mainly a political allegory. In the novel, Rushdie presents the parallel political events going through the consciousness of Saleem Sinai as well as with national history. We have the gruesome account of Jallianwala Bagh massacre by General Dyer, the rule of Congress party in India, language riots between Gujarati and Marathi speaking people in Bombay, the Indo-China War in 1962 leading to a crushing defeat of the Indian Armed Forces, Pakistani Election in 1964, the Indo-Pakistan war over Kashmir in 1965; the house arrest of Sheikh Mujibir Rehman for his demand for an Independent Bangladesh in 1971, the armed conflict between India and Pakistan leading to the liberation of Bangladesh in 1971 and the declaration of Emergency in India by Indira Gandhi which brought the adverse verdict against her election by the Allahabad High Court in 1975. Saleem Sinai, who is both a participant and a witness to many of the above events directly, can transform through his telepathic powers some of them indirectly as he is able to skip backward and forward through time. None of the allegories as mentioned by Rushdie runs throughout the novel. References to mythical characters and events occur here and there and quite a few of them are allegorical regarding contemporary moral or political realities. However, they are presented in fragments not through a medium of continuous allegory which is different from R.K. Narayan's *The Man Eater of Malgudi*, Mulk Raj Anand's *Gauri*, or Raja Rao's *Kanthapura*. Rushdie's use of myth, historical facts and socio-cultural reality of the period in the novel are exquisite examples of unique unity in every respect. By using myths, Rushdie is successful in presenting contemporary events against the background of the universal and the eternal and is able to analyze the complex nature and movement of history of the Indian sub-continent.

A. S. Rao considers *Midnight's Children* as a unique Indian English novel of Postmodern era. He comments: "The earlier novelists like Raja Rao in his *Kanthapura* and Manohar Molgonkar in his *A Bend in the Ganges* also treat the theme of freedom struggle. Khushwant Singh's *A Train to Pakistan* deals with the theme of partition and partly covers post-Independence history of India. But Rushdie's *Midnight's Children* is unique as it puts the same events in singular terms."[12] The novel is a fine combination of history, myth and fantasy which manifests his encyclopedic knowledge as well as the insightful vision of the novelist.

The novel *Midnight's Children* can be categorised into several categories of literary fiction, which include magical realism, post-colonial fiction, and post-modern literature. Therefore, Rushdie's work is often compared to, and is admittedly influenced by novels like Gunter Grass's *Tin Drum* and Gabriel Garcia Marquez's *One Hundred Years of Solitude*. He had equally incorporated the mythical and fantastical elements into his fiction which had uniquely contributed to the English language. Rushdie's inspiration, drawn from both ancient and contemporary Indian culture, is also a notable contribution to Indian English fiction. The novel appears to be a complete history of the life and character of the subcontinent. C.D Narasimhaiah has rightly commented on him:

> Rushdie's Islamic inheritance lets him use the fantasy of the *Arabian Nights*, a children's classic to ignoble ends. He used it with contemporary history, not to illuminate it – he abdicates his role as historian by not caring for facts and violates his vocation as writer because his sole concern is to invite attention to himself with a gusto as to how smartly an Indian could use English language![13]

In *Midnight's Children* and *Shame*, Rushdie has presented the world with certainty and with the most incisive treatments of English fiction of the Indian sub-continent since E.M. Foster's *A Passage to India*. He has also signified the academic world of India which proved a suitable textual example of post-modernist criticism in the field of the contemporary novel. As a Post-Colonial fiction, the novelist treats the period of Indian political history when India became free from the clutches of the British rule and aftermath scenario of Indian past. The novel as a post-colonial text has broken down the national and geographical boundaries and has made it a universal text of human history. Aadam Aziz, a typical Indian Muslim, becomes westernized after his medical education in Germany and turns into an atheist. Though Saleem is brought up in an orthodox Muslim family yet he is half-Hindu and half-Muslim. Since he is brought up by his Christian Ayah, Mary Pereira, he also imbibes and shares something of her faith also. As a result, he compares himself with the legends and myths of all these religions. Alienation emerges as one of the features of post-colonial fiction. Saleem Sinai suffers from alienation and feels deprived of in the end of the novel while all the members of his family are wiped out in Indo-Pakistan war for liberating Bangladesh. *Midnight's Children* reflects the post-colonial hybridism through conflict of cultures as well as political roots. Free India is a new political child or 'twice born' out of indigenous India and that of British Colonial rule.

Rushdie in another novel has also fantasized about Pakistan, it would not be out of context to point out his portrait of the land of the pure country which is "God-ridden country" (p. 350) as described in the present novel. The conditions in Pakistan has stirred his soul and he is forced to declare value judgement which is something very unusual for the narrator:

> In a country where the truth is what it is instructed to be, reality quite literally ceases to exist, so that everything becomes possible except what we are told is the case; and may be this was the difference between my Indian childhood and Pakistani adolescence - that in the first I was beset by an infinity of alternative, while in the second I was a drift, disoriented, amid an equally infinite number of falseness, unrealities and lies. (p. 389)

The novel is a cris-cross of fantastic ironies as well as ironical fantasies. But Saleem is no cynic and is deeply interested in humanity and the men and women around him. He loves life and freedom of people and society and ridicules whatever is outdated, narrow and restricting. As a Muslim, he mocks at the paraphernalia of prayer and sympathizes with his grandfather's decision who is, "unable to worship a God in whose existence he could not wholly disbelieve." (p. 6) He also makes the fun of the 'purdah' system particularly in the episode of the perforated bedsheet and appreciate the courage of his grandmother's unorthodox decision to take up gemstone business while his grandmother sits "hidden behind the veil which the stroke had dropped over his brain" (p. 7) The hatred for narrow-minded communalism is in his family as his grandfather threw out a tutor who taught bigotry and hatred to his children and observed fast for keeping his decision. Thus, we can find that the superficial objectivity in narrative perspective mixed with ironies are woven into threads of sincerity and love which encompasses the whole of mankind.

The narrator is not a "lucid reflector" but "a bizarre refractor of reality" which facilitates our understanding of the contemporary society on the basis of historical events, modes and figures with a touch of comic, moral, humane and cosmopolitan approach.

The novelist reconstructs the fictional reality by using, 'a necessary illusion' and makes it the popular genre of novel. His techniques to achieve such end resort him to a post-modern novel that K.R. Rao calls as "Handcuffed to History" and thus comments on the novel:

> What makes his fiction 'autocthonous' is its awareness of the global history of the sub-continent and its narrative technique which combines the elements of magical realism and the sociology of culture, parody and fastasy with, what Henry James calls the 'inclusive consciousness'.[14]

The novel presents the post-independence political scenario on the pattern of post modern novel. The novelist has skilfully unified myth into history and thus designed the structure of the novel.

Myth plays a vital role in achieving the ironic heights in the text which is subjected to subversions. Myth affects the multistructural meanings in the text by arousing a number of perceptions and responses:

> And there are so many stories to tell, too many, such excess of interwined lives, events, miracles, places, rumours, so dense a commingling of the improbable and the mundane, I have been a swallower of lives; and to know me, just the one of me, you will have to swallow the lot as well (p. 9).

Roger Fowler relates the essential relationship between the structure of the novel and the language used in it and comments:

> The structure of a novel and whatever it communicates are under the direct control of language and concomitantly, of the reader's recreative sympathy, his desire and ability to realize and release the technique from verbal clues deposited by the author.[15]

In brief, Rushdie's *Midnight's Children* is a beautiful tapestry of myth, history, family saga and fable with his master art of fiction writing. As a master artist, his use of myth makes the text of the novel *par excellence*. He tells a story within a story mixes history with allegory and myth and thus cultivates the mythic labyrinth which makes *Midnight's Children* as a superb post-colonial text of world literature.

REFERENCES

1 A.S. Rao: *Myth and History in Contemporary Indian Novel in English* (New Delhi: Atlantic Publishers and Distributors, 2000), p. 101.

2 William Walsh: "India and the Novel" in *The New Pelican Guide to English Literature*, ed. Boris Food (Harmondsworth: Penguin Books, 1983), Vol. 8, p. 257.

3 O.P. Mathur: "A Metaphor of Reality: A Study of the Protagonist of Midnight's Children", *Indian Political Novel and other Essays* (Allahabad: Kitab Mahal, 1995), p. 68.

4 Salman Rushdie: "Reclaiming a city and a History" Express Magazine (*The Indian Express* March 11, 1984), p. 5.

5 O.P. Mathur: opt. cit. p. 68.

6 Linda Hutcheon: *A Poetics of Post-Modernism* (New York and

London: Routledge, 1988), p.5.

7 Salman Rushdie: *Midnight's Children* (1980; rpt. London: Vintage, 1981), p. 195.

8 Uma Parameswaran: *The Perforated Sheet: Essays on Salman Rushdie's Art* (New Delhi: Affiliated West Press Pvt. Ltd., 1988), p. 32.

9 George Lukacs: "The Ideology of Modernism" in David Lodge, ed. 20th Century Literary Criticism: A Reader (London: Longman, 1978), pp. 465-87.

10 Nagesh Chaturvedi: Indian Myths in Rushdie's *Midnight's Children*, Language Forum (Dec. / Jan. 1993), p. 173.

11 John J. White: *Mythology in the Modern Novel: A Study of the Prefigurative Techniques* (Princeton: Princeton University Press), p. 194.

12 A.S.Rao: Op. cit. p.122

13 C.D. Narasimhaiah: *The Swan and The Eagle* (New Delhi: Vision Books, 1999), pp. 246-7.

14 K.R. Rao: "Handcuffed to History: Rushdie's Narratology", *The Journal of Indian Writing in English*, 22.2 (July 1994): 37-40.

15 Roger Fowler: *Linguistics and the Novel* (London: Methuen, 1977, qtd. Uma Paramashwaran), p. 55.

5

The Circle of Reason: Mythic Paradigm

Amitav Ghosh is the finest writer among those who were born out of the post-Midnight's Children revolution in Indian English fiction[1]. He is one of the most talented, innovative and experimental novelists of the age. His first novel *The Circle of Reason*[2] (1986) marks a break from the traditional themes of Indian Engiish novel and designs the new form and structure of the well-made novel.

The chapter intends to deal with mythic paradigm in *The Circle of Reason.* Ghosh has not used myth so extensively in any other novels as he has used it in *The Circle of Reason.* In his other novels, one can trace only the partial and vague treatment of myth. *The Shadow Lines* deals with philosophical ideas whereas *The Circle of Reason* discusses Upanishadic teachings in a mythic framework.

The Shadow Lines[3] is his remarkable novel and it transcends beyond the narrow categorization of an Indian novel. The story centres around Tridib, the narrator's uncle. Memory of childhood is a major theme of the novel. The novel ends with the mystery of Tridib's voluntary death which is symbolic of his sacrifice for humanity.

In An Antique Land [4] is a novel written to recall the spirit of a world which does not exist. The love that once existed between a Tunician Jewish merchant and an Indian Tribal is overwhelming. It makes us sorry for our world of terrorism, riots and communal discord. In *The Calcutta Chromosome*[5] Ghosh has tried to give an answer to West's monopoly over scientific discoveries and inventions. At glance it looks like science fiction. But its logic remains unparallel in undoing the western sense of superiority. *The Glass Palace*[6] (2000) is basically a novel about European greed and the cruelty of colonization.

Amitav Ghosh's *The Circle of Reason* (1986) deals with Nachiketa myth drawn from *Kathopanishad*. The novel is a unique blending of myth and history. Myth offers itself as a means of highlighting the contemporary socio-cultural reality. The novelist shows the turmoil of modern man who has lived through so many "Technology taught horrors" and "organized" genocides generated by money, power and apathy and yet "has gone on to face the future without bitterness."[7]

The novelist takes into account a vast span of time which begins from the ancient time of the *Upanishads* to the infinite future in order to vindicate man's place in history as well as continuity of his evolution. And he treats the myth of Nachiketa in *Kathopanishad* as the relevant context to his novel. It plays a vital role in mediating and communicating truth of the modernist era. Ghosh's awareness to understand and interpret the modern ethos and sensibility has been required to explore the mythical incidents and characters in the present scenario. He simply describes those conditions which are chaotic in the present day society, without being caught in the catastrophe of the complex web of modern anarchy. Thus he achieves the historical insights for the forces which are shaping the present and future of people and society. These insightful histories definitely help him understand the struggle between the forces of progress and reaction and the cycle of life and decay of the modern world. Justifying the title of the novel, Bala Kothandaraman says, "The title of the novel 'circle' has structural ramifications, not the least of which is subversion of its own ultimate concern-Reason"[8]. *The Circle of Reason* is a book written in defence of reason, logic and rationality. In practical life situations, logic hardly works. Cause and effect is a practical theory in a science laboratory, but in real life, it is ineffective.

The myth taken from the ancient Indian Upanishadic myth

of Nachiketa, son of sage Uddalaka, is known for his perseverance and endurance. He makes incessant efforts to implement the decision of his father, who wishes to send him to Lord Yama. Lord Yama was pleased with the sincere logic of Nachiketa and agreed to the child's wish to impart him the divine knowledge. Nachiketa won the heart of Yama with his commitment for the chosen cause which reflected his dedication and the disinterested action for the desired end. Nachiketa rejects the offer of heavenly boon showered upon him by Lord Yama. The Lord of death experiments to examine the power of endurance and exceptional ability of the young sage. Finally, Lord Yama imparts Bramhajnana to Nachiketa which displays the real nature of 'atman'. He learns how to vanquish death and to free himself from desire which is the root cause of decay and destruction. He feels that desire is like fire. The invisible form of Brahman is visible in the form of 'agni'. Therefore, people worship 'agni' in order to purify the surroundings. The use of carbolic acid instead of 'ghee' to make fire burnt on the death of Kulfi signifies such potential idea in the novel. The Upanishadic teachings thus explain the efficacy of knowing the real nature of all pervading Brahman:

"Mahantam Vibhu matmanam Matva, dhirava Schochati".[9]

The essence of *Kathopanishad* is man's desired salvation from the cycle of birth, death and rebirth[10]. Man is a victim of his ignorance which causes the material pleasure and ignores true knowledge. As a result, he moves like a pendulum in the cycle of life and death. When the dawn of enlightenment strikes at the door of jeeva, this cycle ends and man becomes immortal by triumphing over death.

Alu, the protagonist in the novel, is modern Nachiketa; Jyoti Das is inner light; Zindi is life; Maya is 'Avidya' (ignorance); Balram and Shombhu Debnath are both Reason and Yama, the Lord of Death.

The plot of the novel revolves round the central character Nachiketa Bose, nicknamed as Alu. The mythical Nachiketa spent three nights in the abode of Yama and learnt about the three great qualities – Satwa, Rajas and Tamas which govern the movement of human beings on the earth. Satwas is reason, Rajas passion and Tamas is death, i.e. ignorance which is born out of Maya or Avidya. The story begins when an eight-year-old orphan Nachiketa Bose comes to live with his Uncle Balram Bose in Lalpukar. The orphan's head is extraordinarily remarkable that the novelist calls as "an extraordinarily head, huge, several times too large for an eight year old, and curiously, uneven, bulging all over with knots and bumps." (p. 3) It is Boloi da, who gives Alu his life long name as well as part of his identity, "No, it is not like a rock at all. It's an Alu, a potato, a huge, freshly, dug, lumpy potato. So Alu he was named and Alu he was to remain" (p. 3). On the allegorical plane, Alu is something which is rooted in soil and, it has always its identity. But as he is seen by his tortuous wandering, Alu himself seems satirical to his name.

Balram, Alu's uncle, claims to be a rational figure. He admires scientists like Jagdish Bose, Meghnad Saha and Louis Pasteur. He is obsessed with the science of phrenology. His uncompromising stand on rationality has been his theory of life which wins him a life long friend, Gopal. He also gets associated with a rationalist society. But Gopal, even though his best friend, senses something wrong about him,

> As he watched Balram go, Gopal had a premonition: a premonition of the disaster he would call upon himself and all of them, if ever he is allowed to take charge of society. He decided then, with an uncharacteristic determination, that he would do everything in his power to keep that from happening. (p. 50)

Rationality of Balram is juxtaposed with the premonition of his well-wishers and it shows how contradictory forces work. Premonition comes true but rationality does not die. Balram starts a school in his village which is called 'School of Reason'. Toru Debi teaches sewing and Shombhu Debnath, weaving. The modern Nachiketa, who grows up under the able guidance of his uncle Balram Bose, perceives truth which is present in scientific reasoning. Balram's obsession with reason results in the use of carbolic acid in order to clean the unhygenic surroundings. Carbolic acid is symbolic of cleansing unhealthy and undesirable practices of society. Balram Bose constantly makes an effort to maintain healthy and hygienic conditions in the village and around. He starts the school of Reason with a missionary zeal after resigning his job of school teacher that he runs in the village on the land of village land lord Bhudeb Roy. Roy was displeased when he employs his nephew Alu as an apprentice with Shombhu Debnath, an expert weaver, who is a rival of Roy. Maya is Shombhu's daughter whose affectionate look enables Alu to become the master craftsman. He learns the art and science of weaving swiftly. Shambhu himself educates Alu about the art and craft of weaving.

Balram, a school teacher, acts as Ghosh's mouthpiece when he says,

> It would be wrong; it would be immoral. Children go to school for their first glimpse into the life of the mind. Not for jobs. If I thought that my teaching is nothing but a means of finding jobs; I'd stop teaching tomorrow. (p. 52).

Balram considers education as a tool for cultivating and disciplining mind rather than as an equipment for getting jobs. Being a rationalist, he implements his programme for disinfecting the village by dousing it with carbolic acid. Here reason wins and Lalpukar becomes free of cholera and dysentery while many neighbouring villages fall prey to them. But common sense soon turns into obsession as Balram's feud with Bhudeb Roy regarding carbolic acid becomes an issue, a symbol. For Balram, carbolic acid is used as a tool for men of science in order to destroy germs and bacteria but when Bhudeb Roy opposes such campaign for cleanliness, it becomes a weapon to fight evil with. The conflict is both significant and symbolic as it is the conflict of the symbol of reason and rationality which is being destroyed by the more malignant potency of Bhudeb Roy's weapon. When at last Balram lies dead, surrounded by drums of carbolic acid, we come to know that it is not merely the death of an obsessed old man but it is the death of a symbol also and that of the victory of unreason over reason. But it is also ironical that it is not only Bhudeb Roy's unreason that wins over Balram's rationality but also Balram's reason which is reduced and turned from obsession to insanity.

The novel's early part is essentially concerned with the concept of reason. The conflict between rationality and irrationality continues. Balram, his friend Dantu and Gopal Day represent the forces of reason. The slick students of the city led by Maithili Charan Mishra stand for irrationality. The intellectual discourse of the first generation during college days in the city of Calcutta ends in the life's laboratory of experimental world. The second generation is lead by children such as Alu, Mrs. Verma, who take up respective positions. It highlights the intellectual conflict of old and new generation on the basis of value judgment.

The scene of action shifts to Al-ghazira, an imaginary Gulf city, where Alu is hunted by Jyoti Das who arrives in Al-Ghazira with the help of Zindi. His providential escape from the debris of a collapsed multi-storeyed building 'star'; Kulfi's death, Alu and Zindi returning homeward completes a full circle. Thus myth here applies as a pre-figuration of conflict of action between two generations and of their value considerations. Defining the technique of pre-figuration, John J. White says:

> A myth introduced by a modern novelist into his work can pre-figure and hence anticipate the plot in a number of ways. The myth will offer the novelist a short hand system of symbolic comment on modern events. 'Pre-figuration', is a useful word to describe this relationship, since it suggests coming before and hence offering a comparison with a whole configuration of action and figures.[11]

There is a conscious effort regarding the role of mythical or legendary story for revealing the contemporary situations and value judgments of the existing historical situations of contemporaneity with a touch of irony. Nachiketa is the personification of perseverance while Balram is the embodiment of reason. The relevance of their action in the modern Indian situation is noteworthy. The twin ideas of reason and religion are much debated and discussed in order to reach the full circle of reason. The story is centred round the protagonist Nachiketa Bose, who has a vegetable-like existence.

The Circle of Reason is a picaresque novel which is related to the adventures of Alu who descends suddenly on his Uncle and aunt in Lalpukar after the death of his parents. It ends with Alu returning home after adventure that takes him from his village to the borders of West Bengal via the middle East to Al-ghazira and from there his home coming takes place. But Alu is merely a thread of the narrative joint, which can be divided into two entirely unrelated parts – part one, dealing with Alu's Uncle Balram in Lalpukar and part two with Zindi in al-Ghazira.

Alu loves sewing machine because Toru Devi, the wife of Balram, likes it. She is always preoccupied with the world of sewing machines, Zindi is obsessed with Darban Tailoring House; and Professor Samuel with theories of queues. Alu's fascination for sewing machine tempts to accompany Zindi Westward – Jyoti Das says, "Don't worry about sewing machines, they make them better at homes." (p. 420) The sewing machine that Alu seeks to procure represents "Reason, which makes the world mad and makes it human." (p. 58) Reason in the novel is synonymous with mythical Nachiketa's Brahmajnana which he acquires from Lord of righteousness, Yama.

Alu's journey is an inner voyage as the ships carry him to enlightenment. Alu's quest for truth leads him to the company of Balram where he learns about science that can only talk about the things as they appear but not the real reality. He feels that bookish knowledge is artificial as it cannot satiate man's self. It has no redeeming perception. "The machine had driven men mad." (p. 57) His knowledge of craft of weaving fetches him money and provides him substantial return. But soon he realizes that ignorance is born of 'money' (materialism) which is the cause of death. He becomes aware of the fact that education is no answer to all problems of life and cannot be solved merely through cogitations about the cosmic reality. Experience is more useful than mere classroom education. Experience is the best teacher which can decide the value judgement of life and society:

> Do you remember how Pasteur first came to science? It was not by thinking about the cosmic Atom ... Has anything

> changed the world as much as the discovery of the germ? Has there ever been a greater break in history than the moment when men were unburdened of their responsibility for their bodies and all diseases were assigned to the treachery of the elements? And how did it come about? Not through cogitations about the cosmic, but as an answer to the everyday problems of simple people. (p. 49).

Man does not live by bread alone. His problems require another knowledge in order to resolve day to day problems of life. Man should be a master to understand the myriad aspects of life for developing an all around personality. Carbolic acid, money and sewing machine are the materialistic germs which destroy man. one can see such evidence in the following lines.

> Bhudeb Roy lives in mortal fear; there is nothing in the world that he fears as much as carbolic acid. His whole life is haunted by his fear of antiseptic. He'd do anything, go to any lengths to destroy my carbolic acid. He fears it as he fears everything that is true and clean and a child of Reason. He is closing the school down because he thinks it'll put an end to my work with disinfectants. (p. 100)

Alu's encounter with Jyoti Das, Zindi, Balram and Shombhu help him understand the reality with the help of the teaching of Lord Yama. Like the - mythical Nachiketa, he too comes back home as a liberated being. The experiences that Alu gathers right from the beginning to the end of his journey reflect the process of learning of mythical Nachiketa. Amitav Ghosh dislodges the Upanishadic concept of emancipation and establishes his own concept by accepting the fact that *avidya* is a root cause of misery and ignorance which is born out of money that leads to death. Nachiketa Bose (Alu) knows the truth that is hidden behind scientific reasonings. He wants to apply the scientific approach in removing the ills of the present day society. At last he declares that money (materialism) is the enemy of mankind:

> Pasteur had discovered the enemy, the germ, but he had never been able to find him. All his life he had tried to launch war but, like a shadow, the enemy had eluded him,

> and in the end Pasteur had died defeated and bewildered. Why? Because for all his genius Pasteur had never asked himself the real question: Where is the germ's battleground? What is it that travels from man to man carrying contagion and filth, sucking people out and destroying them even in the safety of their own houses, even when every door and window is shut? Which is the battleground which travels on every man and every woman, silently preparing them for their defeat, turning one against the other, helping them destroy themselves?

That was the real question, and Pasteur had never known it. Then he leapt to his feat and with a sigh the whole crowd rose with him. He shouted in Arabic ... I am his heir, for in the ruins of the star I found the answer. Money. The answer is money. (Pp. 280-81)

He imagines not emancipation but resurrection. Death is an essential part to complete the cycle of life. Knowledge of this truth helps one to cross the threshold of illusion, go beyond to emerge as a new being. Through Alu, the novelist acknowledges the essence of death and illusion. So Alu reads about a passage from the 'Life of Pasteur'.

It's about the death. It says that without the germ 'life would become impossible because death would be incomplete. (p. 396)

Yet hope for betterment as hope never dies.

What Balram, Alu's phrenology – obsessed Uncle tells Alu is significant:

> One ought to think of the future. The future is important. The past does not matter. One can do anything with the future. One can change the world (p. 28) only one has to redress life. Man is neither an absolute God nor is he absolutely diabolic. In fact 'order' and 'chaos' are two sides of the same coin. They are "two halves of one apple ... one raw, one rotten. (p. 141)

What Mrs. Verma opines is actually Ghosh's own attitude

towards life:

> Nothing's whole anymore. If we wait for everything to be right again, we shall wait forever while the world falls apart. The only hope is to make do with what we've got. (pp. 416-17)

The novel is characterized by post-modern self-reflexivity. This is exemplified in the argument of Balram Bose and his friend Gopal, when they are at a melodramatic movie. Balram holds the opinion:

> What you heard is rhetoric, how can rhetoric be real or unreal? Rhetoric is a language flexing its muscles. You would not understand. You have spent too many years reading novels about drawing room in a language whose history has destroyed its knowledge of its own body (p. 53).

Balram's obsession with carbolic acid attracts the attention of police, who, in connivance with the local landlord dub him as an extremist, and tries to eliminate him. His studies on phrenology are erroneous because science cannot solve the problems of life reality which is built on hypothesis. So Balram's predictions are often far from accuracy. Bookish knowledge cannot grant such redeeming perception. Indeed Balram's concepts of the new science were out of date, Curie and Pasteur, being both creators of a new consciousness, are the inheritors of the old. For Balram's reliance on a nineteenth-century pseudo-science, Phrenology, in fact, approximates the Indian 'Superstition' of popular religion and astrology that the novelist opposes. The scene of Toru Devi's burning of Balram's library books is analogous to Yama's commandment:

> This self cannot be known through much study, nor through the intellect, nor through much hearing. It can be known through the self alone that the aspirant prays to ...[12]

In the novel, Ghosh underlines that modern man's life in the twentieth century has become more complex and paradoxical than ever before. The novelist does not decry intellectual and scientific pursuits and uses the metaphor of loom for depicting the predicament of modern man. Man's invention of machine has been compared with loom and it is man's curse, which has made him devoid of aesthetic values. The novelist feels that man's excessive dependence on machines is an evil which has made men parasite and useless. Mechanical man is figured like a loom that the novelist tells:

> Man at loom is the finest example of mechanical man, a creature, who makes his own world as no other can, with his mind. The machine is man's curse and his salvation, and no machine has created man as the loom. (p. 55)

The loom never permits the division of reason. But "When the history of world broke, cotton and cloth were behind it, the mechanical man is in pursuit of his own destruction," (p. 57) says Ghosh while considering the merits and demerits of man's invention of machine. Balram assigns Alu the job of apprenticeship at Shombhu Debnath, the master-weaver, where he learns work at loom under the expert tutelage of Maya and her father Shombhu Debnath and provokes him to learn the art and science of weaving. This is what she says in this context: "This is real work. You will never learn to do it." (p. 71) She asks him to go back home. She further adds, "This is children's work; Children do it when they are light." She advises him:

> This is what you are doing-children's work – even though you have got your hair bursting out of your clothes (p. 72).

Maya's father Shombhu Debnath educates Alu with such inspiring and encouraging words, "the machine, like man, is captive to language." (p. 73) Amitav Ghosh very skilfully handles the situations and highlights the dominance of language which provides the very life spirit with which man lives and controls his environment. Man exploits the natural resources and harnesses them to his advantage with the help of language. Language is a handiwork of science which commands the situations. Speaking about the relevance of words Shombhu Debnath says:

> Words, Words, this village teams with words, yet too few to speak of the world and the machine, such wealth and such oppression; to survive a man must try twice as hard, pour

> out words, whatever comes his way hope ... (p. 74)

The loom is also symbolic of words as "language more words, more metaphor, more idiom than all the world's armies of pen wilders" (p. 74)

Rakhal, Shombhu's son starts manufacturing bombs in the forest with the help of rusty nails, metal scraps, broken razor blades, torn rags and such other things as steel-grey non-descript powder. He works busily filling bottles with powder and scraps, stuffing their necks with rags. Rakhal wishes to earn more money and responds to Alu's questions in this context:

> Make money' he answered, 'there is a good market for them; Because of the war, you know. What war? Said Alu.

Not that one, Rakhal waved a dismissive hand at the eastern horizon beyond bamboos. There is a war in the towns, too. They need bombs. You watch, I shall be rich. (p. 78)

But bomb is a symbol of destruction and terror which brings more money through terrorists. If the energies of such misled young people are mal-channelised and if their basic talent is properly utilized for socially useful purposes, they can transform it into the betterment of society. Alu learns the art and craft of weaving more and more. This occupation fetches him money and provides him substantial and constructive returns. In addition to it, Rakhal, a changed one, becomes a good sales manager and gives up making bombs. His hands have become resourceful and helps Alu earn plenty of money who is capable of weaving good butis with intricate patterns included to convey some message, that is to say, with some motif. The one which is known as the political buti earns him good reputation, and has thematic implications:

> Politics buti, nothing more immediate in the world, for the weak Bhudeb Roy answered the call of the people and mounted a caparisoned elephant and toured Lalpukar and the villages around it to announce his plunge, his nose-dive like – emptying leap into politics. Hundreds of the people followed him racing after the elephant, pushing, jostling, fighting to get at its shit. Elephant droppings make good

manure. (p. 81)

It makes clear that people in politics, especially present crop of rulers, degrade themselves to any mean levels to achieve their political ends against their political ideological leanings.

The novelist tries to say that weaving is an inalienable part of human history. "Weaving is reason which makes the world mad and makes it human." (p. 58) As life is nothing but "a glory history in parts; a story of greed and destruction ... But it is the only history we have and history is hope as well as despair." (pp. 57-58) Shombhu Debnath's 'weaving' is juxtaposed with Toru Devi's 'Sewing': The loom (comparison and love) ties the world together permitting "no division of the world" while the sewing machine is self-centered (materialism), it only pieces separate parts together which can be dismembered by undoing the stitches.

The loom never permits the division of reason. But "When the history of the world broke, cotton and cloth were behind it, the mechanical man is in the pursuit of his own destruction," (p. 57) as Ghosh visualizes. Gopal proposes to write the biography of Balram Bose with the story of reason "Reason rescues man from barbarity" (p. 46) is the motto of rationalists.

Here lies the relevance of highly suggestive title, *The Circle of Reason*. 'Reason' here attains a different connotation, implying also the play of imagination. It is not synonymous with logical argument but it reflects the highest intellect and pure knowledge. The characters in the novel are the representatives of reason and are all ordinary human beings who are trying hard to ameliorate themselves and cure their polluted souls in order to achieve such wisdom. This is the motto of the author himself, "There is nothing wrong with your body – all you have to do cure yourself is try to be better human being." (p. 182)

Ghosh's characters appear to be protean in nature. They change and adopt entirely different dimensions. In the second part of the novel, 'Rajas: Passion' the novelist takes recourse to the Biblical myth and underlines evil begotten out of action for self-contentment. Rajas is the most vulnerable phase of spiritual churning that one has to face before realizing the lofty ideals of sublimation, without which no progress is possible. 'Action' is the bedrock of all healthy progress. It is not only individual but also national and ideological progress of man and society. Machine as a tool of science cannot save humanity.

The cyclic order of moral disasters take place in "Rajas: Passion" section of the novel which is reflected as hatred, jealousy, lust, temptation and betrayal through events and characters.

Sin is suffering as an outcome of evil which is shown in the 'Satwa – Reason' section of the novel. Alu stands for the Jesus figure at the centre which is evident in the following lines:

> There were more and more, all over Alu's body, and the pain drove him to walk farther and farther a field – to the crowds fighting their way out of Sealdah Station to Howrah Bridge, across, and still farther, until sirens were shrieking all around him and he was swept away by crowds pouring out of factory gates. It was then that by some inexplicable turn of fortune Alu did something he had not done before ... (p. 155)

He is the son of God or Christ himself, "I'm his heir" (pp. 155, 157, 168) who bears the brunt of others' sin. Alu the Christ incarnate develops boils and the pains become excruciating with the progress of the action (p. 189) The novel thus is an enactment of Christ's life, even the Resurrection myth too is also translated into the text:

> And still he lived through the fall of that whole building. Apparently this is just hearsay he lay flat on the floor with a huge block of concrete just inches from his chest. It is no exaggeration to say that many people in that situation would have died of shock. And far from being dead, he seemed to have come out a new man altogether (p. 275).

In the third section of the novel 'Tamas: Death' Alu places carbolic acid on the funeral pyre of Kulfi which suggests the subversion of reason. Carbolic water has become as a holy water. Mrs. Verma's efforts to maintain and preserve Indian culture is generally mocked at and still ignobly sneered by Mr. Mishra in the midst of Sahara desert. It displays a battle of wits between them. Mrs. Verma reacts to say:

> What does it matter, whether it is *gangajal* or carbolic acid? It is just a question of cleaning the place is not it? People thought something was clean once, now they think something else is clean. What difference does it make to the dead Mishra? (p. 411)

The advent of science and technology cultivated a big jolt to the history of the world. There is a sea change in the attitude and aptitude of the people all over the world. Consequently it led to the topsy turvy situations of the existing value systems. The pouring of carbolic acid on funeral pyre is in sharp contrast with Balram's concerns of cleansing society of its evil practices that he calls 'evil germs'. In this context it is apt to quote Shyamala Narayan when she expresses her opinion:

> The three gunas are almost irrelevant to the understanding of the novel; which is ultimately concerned with reason, and its symbols, the loom, the sewing machine and the book. [13]

Apart from the above three symbols, others are carbolic acid, money, queues etc. which are significant and strengthen the contextuality of texts.

The novelist weaves a spell binding story which ends with a human note. The last words of the novel "Hope is the beginning" (p. 243) reminds us of the opening page with the arrival of Alu which marks the beginning of the story.

The commitment of Alu to the cause of eliminating germs, which he imbibed from his Uncle, is reflected in his impassioned words, ... absolutely silent listening to hardly more than a boy (Alu) talk and that, too, not in one language but in three, four, God knows how many, a Kichri of words, conscious ... tongues unparalleled and woven together ... for every one understood him perfectly, like their mother's lullabies. They understood him for his voice was only the question. The answers were their own (p. 279).

Alu is always moving with his mission. He successfully realizes his own vision in the works of Professor Samuel's 'queues' and 'files' theory which concretises Alu's endearing and evolving socialistic pattern of society as his dream world. Alu and Zindi also return home while Jyoti Das steps into a new world of birds which is true to his aptitude.

In 'Tamas: Death' section of the novel, Ghosh again returns to the Upanishadic projection of his theme to complete the circle. The novelist realizes that 'ignorance is a poor foundation of belief' (p. 408) and rules and orthodoxies are dangerous to humanity:

> All you ever talk about is rules. That's how you and your kind destroyed everything – science, religion, socialism – with your rules and your orthodoxies. That's the difference between us. You worry about rules and I worry about being human. (p. 409)

Modern people believed in the Godless Universe and have no faith in His Commandments. They have forgotten all the human values and have adopted defiled and perverted style of life. Their manner, behaviour and attitude have become beastly. The contemporary fallacious and rational mind has degraded people and society.

Scientific and technological knowledge has killed the artistic sense of man and has made him a worshipper of wealth. It imposes unwanted and unnecessary rules on man to be followed in day to day life. Man has a body as well as a spirit while Science is only concerned with the body of rules. The novelist tries to convey that modern civilization has become too much logical, rational and mechanical, therefore, modern life has become absurd and superfluous. The novelist realizes that rationality alone cannot solve the intricacy and perplexity of contemporary life. He believes that it is only Upanishadic and scriptural consciousness that can make men ideal and moral. It inspires man to the nobler, better and more refined so that he may realize the presence of God.

Creative imagination is a deviation from the accepted norms. 'Poetry should not mean but be' and the problem should remain in the domain of becoming otherwise the world shall come to an end. *The Circle of Reason* carries out the progress of evil as an evolution of necessity for transacting social differences which create different categories in society. We are playing certain roles against our choices and as Heidegger said, we have to become a victim of such categories available in the world. The best way out is to substitute ourselves from such categories with some other categories. However, that is no solution to our problems of roles as it has become a second nature.

In the words of Aruna Mukhopadhyaya, "*The Circle of Reason* is a saga of evolution. Here no character is perfect. Even Alu has his own weakness. Ghosh here implies that everyone is learning the purpose of existence through trial and error. The novel is a perpetual history of man's positive evolution."[14]

The novelist presents the three gunas – 'Satwa"Reason', 'Rajas: Passion' and 'Tamas:Death" as a cycle of reason. His aim is to show man's progression and retrogression which leads to degradation from the enlightened state of Satwa to Tamas. Professor Samuel becomes the spokesman of the novelist's own self. "This is not the end, only the beginning." (p. 409) The novel makes forward or backward movement which makes beginning as the end. The action of the fictional world begins with 'Tamas' and ends at 'Satwa' and he keeps 'Rajas' in between. Alu begins with avidya (ignorance) and travels through the world of darkness and finally reaches the world of light (knowledge) as his desired plentitude of redemption and realises the 'Satwa', as world of his existence. In real life, he goes back 'home' with Zindi (life) and the newly born Child Boss, the future progeny, carries out the light to the future. The end of *Kathopanishad* too imparts the knowledge of truth. Thus the novel *The Circle of Reason* ends like the legend of Nachiketa which accentuates to know the truth of life in the world. Amitav Ghosh weaves such a captivating allegorical and mythical story which ends with human touch of understanding.

In her critical analysis of the novel Shyamala Narayanan says:

"The *Circle of Reason* reminds us of *Midnight's Children*

in the use of language and realism, yet it is not as powerful because the outer and inner reality are at a low level."[15]

The novel suggests that in the world of ideas and ideologies, attitudes only matter Shubha Tiwari rightly opines that. History is not unchangeable but the way we look at it is changeable. Time in the novel is remarkably fluid and characters in the novel are mad after their theories and ideologies which make them mad, abnormal and uncompromising.[16] Unlike William Golding, Ghosh also avoids petty destruction for the greater cause. It is not death which gives meaning to life but it is a life journey which is larger than death. 'The Circle' identifies death in the form of the horror and sadness which controls the process of evolution.

In brief, *The Circle of Reason* is a journey of progress and change through the world of science that a man has to experience in the society as a life reality. Stories and characters are the holders of such conflict of attitudes which make the novel allegorical and mythical that readers enjoy.

REFERENCES

1 R.K. Dhawan: *The Novels of Amitav Ghosh : An Introduction* (New Delhi: Prestige Books, 1991), p. 11.

2 Amitav Ghosh: *The Circle of Reason* (London: Hamilton Hamish, 1986) All references pertain to this edition of the novel.

3 : *The Shadow lines* (New Delhi: Ravi Dayal Publishers, 1988)

4 : *In an Antique Land* (New Delhi: Ravi Dayal Publishers, 1992)

5 : *The Calcutta Chromosome* (New Delhi: Ravi Dayal Publishers, 1996)

6 : *The Glass Palace* (New Delhi: Ravi Dayal Publishers, 2000)

7 Amitav Ghosh: op. cit., p. 79 The Circle of Reason.

8 Bala Kothandaraman: "Circular Reasoning: Amitav Ghosh's Rhetoric" (Osmania: Journal of English Studies XX, 1989)

9 *The Kathopanishad*, 26th Edn. Iii (Gorakhpur: Geeta Press , Govind Bhavan).

All subsequent references pertain to this edition of *The Kathopanishad* and are given in the text.

10 "Man decays and dies like corn and emerges again like corn", *The Kathopanishad,* 1.6, 19.

11 John J. White: *Mythology in Modern Novel*: 'A Study of Prefigurative Techniques'(Princeton: Princeton University Press, 1971), p. 11.

12 *The Kathopanishad*, i, iii, p. 24.

13 ShyamalaNarayan: "The Structure of Amitav Ghosh's *The Circle of Reason*", Littcrit. (June/Dec. 1988), p. 53.

14 Aruna Mukhopadhyaya: "Collage of Myths" Amitav Ghosh's *The Circle of Reason*", eds. R.S. Sharma & S.B. Shukla, *Studies in Contemporary Literature* (New Delhi: Sarup and Sons, 2000), p. 90.

15 ShyamalaNarayan: "The Structure of Amitav Ghosh's *The Circle of Reason*", Littcrit. (June/Dec. 1988), p. 44.

16 Subha Tiwari: *Amitav Ghosh: A Critical Study* (New Delhi, Atlantic Publishers, 2003, p. 120.

6

The Great Indian Novel: Mythic Texture

Shashi Tharoor's *The Great Indian Novel* (1989) has an encyclopedic range suggesting and commenting upon the historical and political constitution of India. It is modelled on the ancient epic of the *Mahabharata* imbibing its structure and issues. One can perceive its account in Salman Rushdie's *Midnight's Children* (1980), the first Indian novel in English, written in the aftermath of the Emergency, which deals with national history. Tharoor also aims at re-telling national history by associating India's past with her present. Tharoor skilfully uses the story of the *Mahabharata* as told by Ved Vyasa in order to describe the socio-political situations before and after Independence so that it could be the Twentieth Century history of India. The *Mahabharata* reveals the popular perceptions and consciousness of ancient Indians and the characters in the novel stand for virtues and vices which are amply allegorized. The epic raises many pertinent social, secular, and administrative problems which seek foster and promote the values and identifies the understanding which makes the history of Great India. The novelist uses the mythical texture of the ancient epic for foregrounding the timeless present as a part of the continuance of the historical evolution of human history from India's deep past to the present. Myth is employed in the novel as an interpretive tool to discuss the basic truths behind present day political crisis in the light of the mythical characters and situations.

The novelist himself tells how he modelled the text of the novel on the pattern of the *Mahabharata*, which is a household book of the Indian subcontinent.

The Great Indian Novel is an attempt to retell the political history of 20th Century India through a fictional recasting of events, episodes and characters from the *Mahabharata* as I explained in an author's note at the very beginning of the book; its title is not a reflection of my estimate of its contents, but a reference to this source of inspiration (for '*Mahabharata*' after all, can be read to mean "Great India")[1].

In the "Afterword" of the novel Tharoor also admits:

> Many of the characters, incidents and issues in this novel are based on people and events described in the great epic, the *Mahabharata*, a work which remains a perennial source of delight and inspiration to millions in India. I am no Sanskrit scholar and have, therefore, relied only on a highly subjective reading of a variety of English translations of the epic. I should like to acknowledge, in particular, my debt to the versions of C. Rajagopalachari and P. Lal, respectively the most readable renderings of what scholars call the southern and northern rescensions of the work. I have relied greatly on both of them. The fictional version of the novel is, of course, mine alone.

The Great Indian Novel is, in fact, a thrice-told tale. The story of the *Mahabharata* composed by Vedvyasa is narrated by Vaishampayan to King Janmejaya. Vedvyasa is not a narrator. Tharoor takes the challenges of re-telling the Mahabharata in the light of the twentieth century political India. The ancient Indian lore reflects faithfully the real Indian consciousness. Like a true visionary, Tharoor's prophetic eye rolls and readily makes itself available to his narrator V.V. to comment upon the twentieth Century post-colonial worldliness of the situations. The novelist writes:

> In the sense, my novel is about the kind of stories a society tells about itself. In many cultures, myths and epics both contribute to and reflect the national consciousness ... what, I asked myself, would a 20th Century Vedavyasa tell about his India the great event of his time?[2]

The novelist sets out the inevitable changes that went through India after British rule. The novelist has streamlined certain novel trends and issues which focus the events of history which are more than a history. It presents the consciousness of history in the light of myth.

Tharoor's tone of irony and his satiric mode of thinking display his intensity of feeling for his country. He describes the degradation of the values in the society which were preached by the great sages of the country. He is totally against the idea of discussing the value system as a mockery by the westernized Indian intellectuals in the seminar halls and conference rooms who do have less knowledge of history and intellectual and cultural heritage of India:

> I tell them they have no knowledge of history and even less of their own heritage. I tell them that if they would only read the *Mahabharata* and the *Ramayana*, study the Golden Ages of the Mauryas and the Guptas and even of those Muslim chaps the Mughals, they would realize that India is not an underdeveloped country but a highly developed one in an advanced state of decay.[3]

The novelist interprets myth and connects it with reality of present day life. Mythic and legendary characters are the rich resources for contemporary Indian writers and the *Ramayana* and the *Mahabharata* are the perpetual fountains for the writers for which Shashi Tharoor's *The Great Indian Novel* is no exception.

The Great Indian Novel apart from being a novel of national history has some resemblance with *Midnight's Children*. *The Great Indian Novel* is a sequel to the advent of new Indian novel in the tradition of *Midnight's Children*, a brilliant account of a great genius. As Viney Kirpal observes in her article "Politics and Philosophy in *The Great Indian Novel*:

> It has the same wide political, historical, geographical sweep, the same interwinning of the individual and the history of the nation; the same audacious re-reading of tradition and history. Again its inventiveness and brilliant word play, the daring experimentation, use of parody and humour and energetic manipulation of English language sets it apart from the earlier English novel.[4]

Viney Kirpal presents the matter of 'intextuality' as a comparative study of Rushdie's *Midnight's Children* and that of Shashi Tharoor's *The Great Indian Novel*. If *Midnight's Children* is about 'broken promises', *The Great Indian Novel* is about 'betrayed expectations'. Both the novels aim at achieving an animated correspondence between myth and reality and hybridise history, myth, autobiography, fiction, non-fiction, fantasy and song into one in a comic burlesque manner. Dealing with the same period of Indian history, both the novels highlight the common events like Jalianwalabagh massacre, partition of India, war with China and Pakistan, Bangladesh war, and the horrors of Emergency. The above events are presented by Shashi Tharoor in a stream of consciousness style of James Joyce and the novelist appears as an Indian James Joyce in presenting the political events of Indian national history. He could not help his anxiety of influence as we can find in the explicit reference of Rushdie's novel made by Vedvyas. While recalling the glories of the attainment of Indian Independence in 1947, Rushdie refers to Ganesha, "Children being born at inconvenient time of the night who would go on to label a generation and rejuvenate a literature". (p.239)

Among other Indian masterpieces, Gandhiji's *Autobiography* and Jawaharlal Nehru's *Discovery of India* and *An Autobiography* serve as source material for Tharoor. Gandhiji's first duel with the crown and the Motihari episode are graphically narrated in *Autobiography* which is an unmatchable piece of literature. In comparison, Tharoor's description of the same event in Book 2 does not possess the same clarity and effectiveness as we find in the first half of the novel which concentrates on Gandhiji and is heavily drawn from Gandhi's *Autobiography*. His lofty idea about the stature and significance of the father of the nation has been obviously influenced by Nehru's views. Tharoor works out in detail on two important remarks made by Nehru, "which revived ancient and forgotten memories and gave her (India) glimpses of her own soul.[5]

Linking Gandhiji to Indian mythology, Nehru said,

Indian mythology is full of stories of great ascetics, who, by the rigour of their sacrifices and self-imposed penance built up 'a mountain of merit' which threatened the dominion of the larger gods and upset the established order. These myths have often come to my mind when I have watched the amazing energy and inner power of Gandhiji coming out of some inexhaustible spiritual reservoir".[6]

In Tharoor's novel, it is the figure of Gandhi (Ganga Datta) with whom the mythic setting of the novel begins and gradually the novel gets "populated by contemporary characters transported incongruously through time to their oneric mythological setting". (p. 355) The portrait of Nehru as sketched in the novel is presented ironically and he is equated with the blind Dhritarastra.

Tharoor cultivates a passage between the modern and the ancient India through the use of the mythical technique. The novelist thus transforms the ancient myth into contemporary politics. It is evident in the following textual quote:

> We Indians cannot resist obliging the young to carry our burdens for us, as you well know, Ganapathi, shouldering mine. So they asked educational institutions, the schools and colleges to mark the centenary, as well with more speeches, more scholarly forums, but also parades and marches and essay contests for the little scrubbed children who had inherited the freedom Gangaji had fought so hard to achieve. (p.46).

In the first quarter of the novel, Vedvyas offers a number of reasons as a source of motivation behind the narrative. He wants to modify the idea held abroad about India as an underdeveloped nation and he emphasises that India is "a highly developed one in an advanced state of decay." (p.17) The contrastive picture, given in the novel, of Hastinapur of the golden past presents the narrator's distrust of the golden past of Hastinapur and finds it as the mythical image of Hastinapur is the ironic description of the narrator in the novel.

Tharoor, however, shows that modern India has been turned into a muddle by her selfish and power-hungry politicians who are called as the modern Kauravas, who wreaked the glorious tradition of India as representated by Bhisma on the one hand and Gandhiji on the other. The narrator in Tharoor's novel says, "History ... indeed the world, the universe, all human life and so every institution under which we live-is in constant state of evolution". (p.245) The novel tells India's story of colonialism and its bitter experiences by transforming the ancient myth into contemporary politics. Tharoor contextualises the *Mahabharata* of yester years with his 'Mod *Mahabharata*' which is the present day Indian political history.

The novel teaches us that the battle of Kurukshetra is within, not without and it is an endless struggle of life. The novelist says, "Life is Kurukshetra", "History is Kurukshetra" (p.391). The modern Vedvyasa, the narrator of the story, elaborates,

> The struggle between dharma and adharma is a struggle of nation, and each one of us in it engages in one single day of our existence. (p.391)

The novel tries to underline the continuance of the historical evolution through, the pastness of the present and the presentness of the past. Vedvyas tells Ganapathi, "...we are all living in an eternal present in which what was and what will be is contained in what is" (p.163). It requires the wisdom of a sage, he tells, to understand the process of history. The history of post-independent India is a reflection of what was the battle of Kurukshetra. Voice against Vedvyas's view is highlighted in Ancient Indian epic battles which were fought for great causes of humanity for dharma and adharma, while in modern India "mediocrity reigns", "dishonesty is the most prevalent art", and "power is an end in itself rather than means, where the real political issues of the day involve not principles but parochialism" (p.412) Vedvyas, on the other hand, focuses the two aspects of the epic age which are divided between, good and bad, which is also a common phenomenon of the modern times. Commenting on the Vedic religion, he says, "our philosophers try to make much of our great Vedic religion by pointing out its spiritualism, its pacifism, its lofty pansophism; and they ignore, or gloss over its superstitions, its inequalities, its obscurantism" (p.412) Vedvyas refuses to accept that the epic warriors died on the mythological battlefields.

The novel is a critique of India's inherent meaningfulness as a human society before the world. Bhisma is figured as a modern Gandhi while Nehru is portrayed like the blind King, Dhritarastra, who inherited the throne on a vow taken by Ganga Putra Bhisma, and here Gangaji stands for Gandhiji. Indira Priyadarshini is figured as Priya Dur, odhani of the novel.

Through the figures of Gandhiji and J.P. Narayan, the novelist tries to interpret that the present history of the country, too, is an epic battle which has been fought for great causes like freedom and democracy. Ancient Hastinapur also contained midnight's parents like Dhritrastra and Karna; mean minded separatists like Duryodhana whose ambition and ego brought about the great devastation and that of dishonest men like Shakuni and tyrants like Jarasandha. The freedom movement and the uprise of the people against Mrs. Gandhi's tyrannical rule mark the continuance of the battle between dharma and adharma. Vedvyas deceptively says that in this confused time he "can no longer distinguish between right and wrong, real and unreal." (p.413) But in the last section of the novel, the Swargarohan Parva, when Yudhisthir expresses his surprise at the sight of Duryodhani enjoying the pleasures of heaven, yama corrects him saying, "It was all an illusion, my son. You will no more be condemned to an eternity of misery than Duryodhani will enjoy perpetual contentment" (p.417) Sinners are given a brief stay in heaven and thereafter they are perpetually condemned to hell. It reverses the good men. Dharma (Yama) asserts,

> Everyone finds his place in history, even those who have failed to observe dharma. But it is essential to recognize virtue and righteousness, and to praise him who, like yourself, have consistently upheld dharma. (p.417).

The history of dharma and adharma decides everybody's role in making the history of nation. Yudhisthir, however, disagrees with the fact that there have been varied and conflicting interpretations of dharma at the different stages of its evolution, as a result, a unitary or single interpretation of the term is not valid and relevant for all ages. But Yudhisthir's, suggestion, "Let each man live by his own code of conduct, so long as he has one" (p.418) is not free from dangerous consequences. He is not clear about "the basic values of the people-those which do not change" (p.418) creates a point of conflict. The novel ends with uncertainty when Vedvyas wakes up from dream to "an India beset with uncertainties, muddling chaotically to the twenty-first Century" (p.418). But the longing continues and the novel closes with a beginning.

The novel reflects Indian ethos and the subversion of myth is the novelist's narrative strategy which includes the cultural, socio-political and linguistic components of the narrative as M. Sivarama Krishna writes:

> The fundamental narrative of a culture (of which later narratives however radical they seem, are only configurations) is a product of its ontology. Its basic modes of perception crystallized in its broad world view are determinants of its narrative structure. If narrative is essentially the way in which all modes of perception embody themselves, then the philosophical, ethical, religious as well as socio-political and linguistic assumptions of a culture are vital components of narrative, whether these are products of their inner indigenous dynamics or their interplay of the question begging but convenient binary of tradition and modernity[7].

Tharoor uses myths both vertically and horizontally. His use of myth is more vertical than horizontal because he gives more emphasis on certain characters than events or situations. He works out the idea of the eternal present by using two separate time-frames, one for the epic age and the other for the modern. He integrates them into a single fold presenting some of the characters, events and situations of the *Mahabharata* and make them contemporaneous and uptodate. By placing the past vertically on the horizontal present, he integrates a number of key episodes of the *Mahabharata* into the story, a couple of which are slightly modified, which aims to project important political events of the post-independent period.

The binary approach of tradition and modernity is figured as it foregrounds the major characters like Gangaji, Dhritarastra,

Duryodhana, Dharmaraj, Karna, Pandu Raj and Draupadi. Tharoor's treatment of characters and events is ironic. Among the characters, the most important is that of Draupadi Mokrasi, who is like the Indian Democracy and is husbanded by like many Pandavas of Janata Party founded by Lok Nayak Jaya Prakash Narayan and led by Morarji Desai. Morarji Desai is like an idol of Dharmaraja in the novel. The novelist describes Draupadi Mokrasi as a symbol of Democracy, the seat of power, and its beauty attracts the power-hungry politicians as the beauty of Draupadi creates the magical effect on her lovers. Such binary comparison of beauty of Draupadi with Democracy is the noteworthy contribution of the novelist:

> Draupadi's beauty attracted both men and women, both young and old. All sought to be part of her beauty; no man presumed to attempt its submission ... She was like the flame of brass lamp in a sacred temple of the people. Imagine it: a flame nourished by a ceaseless stream of sanctified oil and the energy of a million voices raised in chanting adoration. A flame at an evening aarti, at the end of the Puja, a flame offered to the worshippers as bells tinkle and incence smoke swirls, and a hundred hands reach out to receive its warm benediction; a flame curling and moving towards these hands, glowing ever more brightly as it breathes these hands, glowing ever more brightly as it breathes their reverence. This was the beauty of Draupadi, a beauty that glowed in the open that drew sustenance from the public gaze. The more people behold her, the more beautiful she seemed. (p. 309).

The novelist presents a vivid image of the evening puja, and the image serves to stress the importance of religion in the Indian democracy.

The description of Mohammed Ali Karna, who is an image of Jinnah and whose career begins in politics as a member of Kaurava Congress Party, is quite amusing. He is as bright and resplendent as the sun. He is the son of Kunti Devi by Hyperion Helios, the wandering magnate of the sky. Tharoor delves deep into the details of circumstances of his birth as well as the reasons for his alienation from Congress Party which compelled him to join Muslim League for cultivating the equation between Karna and his modern leadership.

Karna as an ill-fated and powerful warrior emerges on the Kaurava political scenario and he comes out of nowhere. It is a beautiful tapestry of the novel by comparing Karna with Jinnah:

> Few things were known about this strange young man whose words glowed like his skin, who maintained a most un-Indian reticence about his origins, his family, his native place... He first came to national attention as a flourishing lawyer in Bombay, sharp, suave and self-assured with a bungalow on Malabar Hill and an accent to match the cut of his Savile Row suits... He lived alone, seemingly parents, friends, a background such as all Indians take for granted. (p.136)

He resigns from the Kaurava Congress party and is unable to stand the gibes of Dhritarastra, Nehru and the pompous secularism of Mahatma. He joins the violently theocratic Muslim Group. Prem Nanda Kumar appreciates the depiction of Karna's character and says :

> Vyasa's Radheya Karna and Tharoor's Mohammed Ali Karna run on identical parallel tracks, thanks to Tharoor's exuberant imagination. Our new Karna's rise is every bit of it enjoyable (if terrible) drama.[8]

Other important mythical characters like Gangaji are also subjected to severe ironic touch. The description of Ganga Dutta going to the forest with his guests to meet the head fisherman and ask the hand of Satyavati for Shantanu serves as an illustration,

> Ganga Dutta did not travel alone either. In later years, he would be accompanied by a non-violent army of Satyagrahis, so that the third class train carriages he always insisted on traveling were filled with elegantly sacrificing elite of his followers, rather than the sweat stained poor, but on this occasion, it was a band of ministers and courtiers, he took with him to see Satyavati's father. Ganga D would always have a penchant for making his most dramatic gestures before a sizeable audience. One day he was even to die in front of a crowd. (p.23)

Gandhi serves as the greatest linking factor between the past with the present, "reading *Vedas* and Tolstoy with equal involvement, studying the innumerable laws of Manu and the eccentric philosophy of Ruskin" (p.25) The first half of the novel establishes a close parallel between Bhisma and Gandhiji which begins from the taking of the terrible vow to the agony of the partition and that of the final assassination.

The modern Dhritarastra, Jawahar Lal Nehru, "had the blind man's gift of seeing the world not as it is, but as he wanted to be".(p. 85) In the context of Dhritarastra Nehru's western ways, Shashi Tharoor says :

> Dhritarastra was a fine – looking young fellow, slim, of acquiline nose and aristocratic bearing. His blindness was, of course, a severe handicap, but he learned early to act as if it did not matter. As a child he found education in India a harrowing experience, which was no doubt, why he was in due course sent to Eton. The British Public School System fitted the young man to a T (the finest Darjeeling, which he obtained every month from Fortnum and Mason) and brewed several times a day in a silver pot engraved with the Hastinapur crest (p. 41).

The myth of Nehru as the 'leader of the Nation' is highlighted ruthlessly, and it is no less than that of Mahatma 'the Father of the Nation'. The same ironic vein continues every inch in the novel. Commenting on the Dhritrarastra-Gandhari's marriage, the novelist writes which "made a strange pair, those two - the blind patrician and the blind politician" (p. 229).

Tharoor selects the events cautiously and portrays them with meticulous care. He tailors them according to the needs of modern India with all its ambivalences, ambiguities and colours the fragmented psyche of the nation. The dramatization of the text produces ideology. Thus the novelist writes a history of ideology, which is of oppositional kind to construct the Gandhi-Nehru framework of politics which played the dominant role on the political scene of Post-independent India. Frederic Jameson truly concretises the problem of the political interpretation of literary texts of the novel which is relevant :

The book will argue the priority of the political interpretation of literary texts. It conceives of the political perspective, not an auxiliary to other interpretive methods current today … but rather as the absolute horizon of all reading and all interpretation."[7]

Subhas Chandra Bose, the modern version of Pandu, is presented ironically but not sympathetically. He is seen as the maker of the history of India. But his nature and character is ironically sketched in an interesting manner:

> … Pandu stayed in India and fretted, while the man he admired, but could not bring himself to surrender everything, crossed his legs on a cold wooden chair and awaited his turn to speak after the Monarchits and the liberals and the society for the Preservation of the Imperial Connection, which had each sent more representatives to the Round Table than the Kauravas. But Pandu, though now bitter in his denunciation of his sightless sibling, was still a loyal party man (p. 115).

The other principal characters of the *Mahabharata* are conceived as the major institutions of India – Bhima as the Army, Arjuna as the press, Draupadi as democracy.

In his fictional treatment of the history of India of the post-Gandhi period, Tharoor uses myth skilfully by relating the Indian past with present dream of India. The defeat of Hidimba by Bhima is used as a parallel for the liberation of Goa from Portugese rule; the tearing off of the body of Jarasandha into two by Bhima reflects the dismembering of Pakistan and the creation of Bangladesh. By replacing Bhima by Sahadeva in the original episode of Bhima – Bakasura wrestling match, the sad and humiliating defeat of India in the Indo-China war has been mirrored. The most effective use of the mythic setting, however, is found in Tharoor's creative use of the episode of the disrobing of Draupadi as a parallel for Mrs. Gandhi's misrule of the country, her overthrowing of democracy and the abrogation of constitutional rights during the Emergency. Disrobing of Draupadi here is symbolical of denuding Indian people of their dignity and freedom. The marriage of Draupadi and Arjuna is given as a modern meaning of a union of democracy and that of the voice of the people through the press.

The modern journalists, the keepers of democracy, are confused and divided like the modern Arjuna who is a journalist, a representative of the powers and weaknesses of the Indian press in the novel. Vedvyas says about him:

> I thought of Arjuna, says Vedvyas, "with his paradoxical mixture of attributes, as the spirit of the Indian people, to whom he so able gave voice as a journalist.

India could not be India without the loud, vibrant, excited babel of contending opinions that its press expresses. Arjuna, himself a man of contradictions, perfectly reflected both the diversity and the discordance of the Indian masses, whose collective heartbeat he heard and echoed. His gentleness of express, his frequently troubled frown of reflection, mirrored the doubts and questions that were as much a part of his nature as the decisive flurries of action he undertook when circumstances generated their own certainties. (p.320).

Arjuna has a vital role to play as a saviour of the nation from political tyranny and oppression. The Pashupat Astra that he receives from Lord Shiva, symbolizes the power of the press in democracy. It is the 'ultimate weapon' which he has to use with discretion and not only for devastation but also for construction. Arjuna is seen as a worshipper of Agni, the god whose hunger is satisfied by him by setting Dandakaranya on fire (the great forest fire), "Give us Agni the power to create as we have strength to destroy." Agni's reply has a Mephistophilisian echo, "you shall have it but not yet" (p. 358).

The novelist believes in the power of press and it has played the significant role in highlighting the atrocities of emergency till it came to an end. The national hero of Independence Subhash Chandra Bose is equated with Pandu Raja, who died a premature death. Mohammed Ali Karna's (Jinnah) feeling of alienation in the Kaurava Congress Party drives him to desperate action of creating the partition of India. He gets treatment of real Karna who was neglected by Kuru Pandavas becaue of his low birth as

Suta putra. The comic mode of narration in the novel is evident in the following lines:

> History, Ganapathi, indeed the world, the universe, all human life and so too, even institutions under which we live is in a constant state of evolution. The world and everything in it is being created and recreated even as I speak, each hour, each day, each week going through the unending process of birth and re-birth, which has made us all. India has been born and reborn again, India is forever, and is forever being made. (p.62)

The metaphysical statement makes a sad commentary on the deterioration of ethical, moral values in the public life of the country which is reflected through rampant corruption, senseless violence in the form of communal riots and disruptive activities taking place in every nook and corner of India.

Priya Duryodhani is the modern model of Indira Gandhi. The novelist writes about her in an ironic manner :

> Priya Duryodhani acted only according to the dictates of her own conscienceless mind. Even at the age of twelve, overkill was already her problem. (p.155).

In the portrait of modern Drona, Jaya Prakash Narayan, Tharoor makes a free use of myth in the epic story. Drona sided with Duryodhana supports his employer, but his modern figure fights against Duryodhani for the sake of truth and justice. It raises the question if the modern Drona is greater than the original one. Such interplay of the story with the epic jeopardizes our idea of the epic characters. Besides, such forced equations with the strong pornographic elements in the amorous scenes, particularly in the case of Vyabhichar Singh with the French woman, has little justification. It seems that the novelist occasionally plays the fictional art for creating the sheer pleasure in it.

In *The Great Indian Novel*, every prominent member of the epic, the *Mahabharata*, is allegorized for the novelist's needs for the political narrative. Everybody represents some contemporary historical personage with some singularities or angularities attached with one's personality. The novelist exposes that politics has the dubious nature which is mirrored through the political circles in the novel and that of the country. Viney Kirpal rightly comments on the novel:

> Tharoor's interpretation is a successful comment on the present day Indian elite raising on the backs of their more unfortunate brethren. Thus, through a multi-layered treatment, the novelist both questions the ethics of tradition and evokes the essential *Mahabharata* to understand the persistent orthodoxy in present day India.[10]

The novel evokes the political unconsciousness shrouded behind all major political events of pre and post-independent India. It begins with unity and diversity mission of political leaders during freedom struggle and ends with partition situations. It dwells upon the state of the enthusiasm and euphoria, instant post-independent days and ends with the period of utter misrule of Emergency.

Tharoor expresses his greatest anguish at the disappointing turn of events in Independent India which has shattered the dreams of the founding fathers and betrayal of the hopes of the masses who pinned up their faith in the leaders. It is, in a way, an expression of 'general angst', which gives vent to their dismay and despair at the failure of their masters. The novel breaks off in 1980 when Priya Duryodhani once again assumes the reigns of the country after her triumphant return to power. *The Great Indian Novel* ends with the words wherefrom it has begun:

"They tell me India is underdeveloped country" (p.17)

The twentieth century waits another Vyasa-voice. According to P. Lal :

> For Peter Brook the relevant Vyasa-voice was one that Iravati Karve in her brilliant sociological and psychological study of the epic, titled Yuganta. She treated the *Mahabharata* as a narrative describing the end of yuga; it is a Dooms Day History, by thus 'repeating' itself, is teaching us lessons it would be foolhardly to ignore.[11]

The above observation shows the stupendous attempt of

Tharoor's re-writing of the ancient Indian epic into allegorical, mythical and political implications of the national history of India. The novelist successfully attempts the new political paradigm and testifies the concept of 'Dharma' which is the constant struggle within human psyche. He also questions the sense of justice and sympathises with saga of the sacrifices of common folk, who are alive to serve their new masters in Independent India even after breaking the shackles of their alien masters in the past:

> They did not starve to death, because they slaved and swept and sowed and stood and served and scratched in order to slake the hunger in their bellies, and found just enough to keep alive – underfed, undernourished, undergrown, underweight, underclad, undereducated, under active, underemployed, undervalued and underfoot, but alive. (p. 357).

The novelist is a master artist of parallelism which de-familiarises the political personalities and their issues and treats them at the realistic plane of his novel-writing which ranges from the epic age to the modern times. "The purpose of parallelism", according to Victor Shklousky is, "like the general purpose of imagery, is to transfer the usual perception of an object into the sphere of new perception that is, to make a unique semantic modification."[12] The novelist's parallelism has a unique art of semantic modification which centralizes the truth and which has become a universal truth that 'history is Kurukshetra'. (p. 391).

The novelist shows that history is not only blind like Dhritarastra but it also repeats itself. At the end of the novel, Yudhisthir, the original one, tries to find liberation from the bondage of history. For him, it is tested on the touchstone of time which decides the role of man in history. *Dharma* and *Adharma* are the two balances of time which fix the role of man in the life of the nation and which continue a perpetual Kurukshetra. It had been the source of the conflict and solution in the past and also in the present.

The novel ends with a note of uncertainty by the narrator who wakes up from dream and tells "an India beset with uncertainties, muddling chaotically to the twenty-first Century." (p. 245)

In the novel, we may find that the novelist has made both implicit and explicit use of myths. In James Joyce's *Ulysses*, there is an implicit use of myth and Tharoor wrote *The Great Indian Novel* on the pattern of Joyce's Ulysses, he has also made a selective use of myth. The novel is not fully based on the story of the *Mahabharata* as some of the events and characters are not discussed. The battle of Kurukshetra is omitted. The game of dice is played in dream. Some characters like Eklavya, Aswasthama are fully changed. But for Indian readers, who are fully aware of the story of the *Mahabharata*, there is an explicit use of myth in the novel. They co-relate the story of the *Mahabharata* with the story of the novel and establish parallel. In this sense the use of myth seems to be explicit. Some of the characters like Draupadi Mokrasi, Mohammed Ali Karna, Ganga Dutta and Morarji Desai are the modern mythological models while there are some historical figures like Draupadi, Jinnah, Gandhiji and Dharmaraja who come under a cyclic pattern.

In the words of C.D. Narasimhaiah, "If Rushdie is a juggler of words, Shashi Tharoor is a juggler of myths. He uses the *Mahabharata* story recklessly to mediate contemporary political experience. He establishes reckless correspondences between contemporary political figures and the characters in the *Mahabharata*. But one's understanding of the novel is in proportion to one's acquaintance with all that they stand for. And to one who knows the correspondences Tharoor can only cause exasperation. If that is so for an Indian how does an outsider sort out the relationships? The book is a madhouse in which only his publishers, Penguine India, must have seen merit. If Tharoor didn't mention certain persons or events in the history it is because, for him, they 'didn't matter'. And finally he confesses unforgivably 'I have told my story from a completely mistaken perspective'. And so convinces Ganapathi who becomes a recorder – that he is left with no choice – a concession he bestows on Vyasa's character who is also a recorder. He must 'retell it', he vows. One only hopes he will not. Enough of the liberties he has taken with the epic which he reduces to a caricatuse."[13]

The novelist claims to present in his novel "an idea of multiple realities" and "the multiplicity of truth" (p. 418). The novel suggests that by accepting diversity alone, India can escape from the mistakes of the past. In brief, we can say that Shashi Tharoor by re-telling the epic stories of the *Mahabharata* has drawn a mythical parallel of the modern political scenario of independent India. The epical proportions are aptly suggested by Tharoor's *The Great Indian Novel* even though the epic as a genre has been substituted for a narrative that has dramatic elements. Therefore, C.D. Narasimhaiah calls him as "a juggler of myths" which fulfils the dreams of the novelist to display "an idea of multiple realities" prevailing in the life of people and society in India. To some extent, it is a critique of Indian politics in *The Great Indian Novel* which is both a novel as history and history as a novel where his use of myth becomes a tool of literary art. Myth is timeless and it can telescope time and make it cyclic and eternal. Therefore, the history of epic has also become the history of modern India. By using myth in *The Great Indian Novel*, Shashi Tharoor becomes a fine example of myth-making novelist in Indian English narrative tradition.

REFERENCES:

1. Shashi Tharoor : "Yoking Myth to History", Littcrit (Dec., 1990), p. 5.
2. *Ibid.*, p. 5.
3. Shashi Tharoor: *The Great Indian Novel* (New Delhi: Penguin Books India, 1989) p. 17. All subsequent references pertain to this edition of the novel and are given in the text.
4. Viney Kirpal: "Politics and Philosophy in *The Great Indian Novel*", *Littcrit* (June/Dec. 1990) pp. 9-12.
5. Jawahar Lal Nehru:*An Autobiography* (New Delhi: Oxford University Press, 1982), p. 254.
6. *Ibid.*, pp. 253-254.
7. M. Sivaram Krishna: "Telling the Stories Indian Way: Indo-English Novel and the Structures of Indigenous Narratives", Osmania Journal of English Studies XXV (1989) p. 164.

8. Prem Nanda Kumar : "Shashi Tharoor's Karna", *Littcrit*, (June/Dec. 1990) p. 17.
9. Frederic Jameson: "On Interpretation: Literature as a Socially Symbolic Act", The Political Unconscious: Narrative as a Socially Symbolic Act; London, 1971, 17.
10. Viney Kirpal: *op.cit.*, p. 48.
11. P. Lal : "Mod *Mahabharata*", *Littcrit* (June/Dec. 1990) p. 10.
12. Victor Shklovsky: "Art as Technique", in *Modern Criticism and Theory: A Reader*, ed. David Lodge (London and New York: Longman, 1988) p. 27.
13. C.D. Narasimhaih: *The Swan & The Eagle* (New Delhi: Vision Books, 1999) p. 247.

7

Conclusion

The preceding chapters focus on myth, its meaning, function and its extensive use in Indian English fiction in general and in the novels of prominent novelists like Raja Rao, R.K. Narayan, Salman Rushdie, Amitav Ghosh and Shashi Tharoor in particular. Their use of myth in the novels suggests the search for truth in their art of story-telling. Unlike history, myth is dateless and timeless and it contextualizes history and makes it relevant to the present. Moreover, history begins with myths. Mythic narrative reveals and continues the archetypal patterns and meanings in contemporary history and it often happens in Indian English novel. One can witness the thematic concerns of the novelists starting from Raja Rao to Shashi Tharoor which have been correlated and contextualized between history and myth. To Indian English novelists, myths reveal inner reality more accurately than scientific discourses. They work like a kind of therapy for the problems of humanity. They can also mirror in their unconscious minds. The use of myths functions like a narrative which characterizes a large part of literature written during the present time.

The mythic mode has become a dominant literary technique since the publication of James Joyce's *Ulysses* (1922). Indian English fiction has its bedrock in Hindu mythology which contextualizes the contemporary times in the realm of politics, morals and culture. Myth is deeply rooted in Indian psyche. A large number of Indian English novelists have based their novels on the Puranic pattern of narrative. The earliest narrative forms taken from the *Puranas* establish mythic narratives. Indian English novelists interpret contemporary India in the light of ancient myths and legends. Like English writers, these Indian novelists also bring out the binary contexts between the past and the present by using myths in varied ways. They highlight the complexity and intricacy of modern life through mythical methods and treat the complexity and chaos of modern life in their works of art.

The Indian English novelists such as Raja Rao, R.K. Narayan, Salman Rushdie, Amitav Ghosh and Shashi Tharoor believe that myth and literature are interlinked and are the suitable aesthetic expressions of man's feelings which can transform their creative imagination in art. Myth can deal with sociological, political and psycho-analytical problems of man and can become a suitable mode of expressing and revealing the facts regarding the predicament of man.

My analysis focuses on the use of myth in Raja Rao's *The Serpent and the Rope* and R.K. Narayan's *The Man Eater of Malgudi*, makes it clear that they are deeply rooted in their Indian culture and represent its ethos. Myth offers them the varied patterns of traditional motifs for evoking the new meanings. *The Ramayana*, *The Mahabharata* and the *Puranas* are the eternal sources from which R.K. Narayan and Raja Rao have derived their organizational patterns in many ways for their creative purposes.

Raja Rao craves for his own Indian mythical past and has dovetailed mythical experiences with the experience of the immediate present. *The Serpent and the Rope* is written on Puranic art of story-telling. The novel has a philosophical colour which exposes the oriental characteristics of India in the light of the edification of the west. In the novel, the recurrent mythical allusion establishes the binary relationship between Radha-Krishna, Satyavan-Savitri, Tristam-Iseult, and it forms the dominant motif in the relationship between Ramaswamy and Savitri. Raja Rao suggests that non-dualistic philosophy is the fundamental truth which highlights India's quest for truth. One can witness that the Indian Vedantic vision and the wisdom of age-old Indian scriptures like the *Vedas*, the *Upanishads* and the *Gita* have become as the well-knit fabric of *The Serpent and the Rope*.

R.K. Narayan has used myth as metaphor in *The Man Eater*

of Malgudi. It is a modern version of the ancient tale of Bhasmasura, a demon. The novelist makes use of a number of other Indian myths in the novel. He intermingles the mythical characters and events with the contemporary reality. The novelist has employed the Bhasmasura myth as a structural parallel in the novel and has used other myths like Rama-Ravana, Mahisasura, Gajendra Moksha in a digressional manner. All the events and characters of the novel are also metaphorically described which establish Narayana's art of novel writing. In *The Man Eater of Malgudi*, the dovetailing of the ancient and the modern emphasizes how an ancient fable can be a mythical metaphor of immediacy and relevance to our own age. Therefore, one can find in *The Man Eater of Malgudi* the most effective and meaningful use of myth.

While interpreting modern India in terms of ancient myths, Raja Rao and R.K. Narayan differ in their use of myth. R.K. Narayan has made an explicit use of myth in *The Man Eater of Malgudi*. His use of myth as analogy and its recurrent formula is mainly concerned with human conduct whereas Raja Rao's use of myth in *The Serpent and the Rope* reveals the collective consciousness of the age. For Raja Rao myth is like a religious ritual and it makes life more meaningful by delving deep into the essence of life.

The post-independent novelists – Salman Rushdie, Amitav Ghosh and Shashi Tharoor are different from their predecessors – Raja Rao and R.K. Narayan in using myth as thought and attitude. They highlight the divided and fragmented India by using myth ironically in their novels whereas pre-Independent novelists – Raja Rao and R.K. Narayan deal with united India and are respectful to ancient Indian myths and legends. They discuss ancient myths through symbols and metaphors whereas post-independent novelists project contemporary history in a mythic pattern which is full of irony and allegory. Their history is a novel history of contemporary times with context of immediate present.

As a realistic historian, Salman Rushdie creates the personal history of his characters which is coloured by the realistic experiences in his art of novel writing. He has experimented the encyclopaedic use of myth in *Midnight's Children*. The oriental and occidental myths used by Rushdie in this novel expand the horizon of his dimensions in dealing with characters and events pertaining to history. His use of a complex pattern of myths can be considered as 'condensation' and 'fragmentation' which explores the face of reality hidden behind thematic as well as structural pattern of the novel.

Midnight's Children is essentially a political allegory. Rushdie's use of myth, historical facts and socio-cultural reality of the period in the form of novel is unique in every respect. Rushdie successfully presents the contemporary events set against the background of the universal and the eternal times. His mythical use of history successfully delineates the complex movement of history of the Indian sub-continent that one can read in the novel.

Amitav Ghosh is one of the most talented, innovative and experimental novelists of the age. *The Circle of Reason* remarkably breaks from the traditional themes of Indian English novel which in form and structure emerges as the well-made novel. In *The Circle of Reason*, Ghosh uses myth as a paradigm and discusses the Upanishadic teachings in mythic pattern. The Nachiketa myth is drawn from *Kathopanishad* which is a unique combination of myth and history. Ghosh understandably interprets the modern ethos and sensibility through the mythical incidents and characters. In the novel, Ghosh emphasizes that modern man's life in the Twentieth Century has become complex and paradoxical owing to scientific growth and materialism. He condemns materialism, mechanism and scientific pursuits. Ghosh tries to convey that modern civilization has become too much logical, rational and mechanical which turns the modern life as absurd and superfluous. The novelist realizes that rationality alone cannot solve the intricacy of contemporary life. Modern Nachiketa like mythic Nachiketa realizes that carbolic acid, money and sewing machine are the germs, which can destroy man. Science can only talk about the things as they appear and not what they really are. Bookish knowledge has no redeeming perception. Ignorance is born out of 'money' which breeds the germ of death. Hence he reminds us of the relevance of Upanishadic teaching, which explains Brahman:

Mahantam Vibhu matmanam matva, dhirona schochati.

(Kathopanishad i, ii, 22)

(The brave and wise one who knows the almighty and all his pervading nature never lament.)

The novelist believes that it is only Upanishadic and spiritual consciousness that can lead to the birth of an ideal man and society.

Tharoor's *The Great Indian Novel* is a textual exposition of the mega text of the Indian tradition which is *Mahabharata*, modelled as it is on the great epic which serves as a framework for various kinds of cross references. He attempts to re-write the national history in the light of India's past and present. He uses the story of the *Mahabharata* told by Vedvyasa for evoking socio-political situations in India before and after Independence. One can find such similarity in the novels of Rushdie and Tharoor. *The Great Indian Novel* is based on the mythical pattern of the ancient epic for foregrounding the eternal present which connects the historical evolution from India's remote past to the immediate present. The novel teaches that the battle of Kurukshetra is never over. "Life is Kurukshetra, History is Kurukshetra" (p.391). Tharoor suggests that by accepting diversity alone India can escape from the mistakes of the past. The novel is not fully based on the story of *Mahabharata*. Some of the events, situations and characters are omitted. The battle of Kurukshetra is also omitted. The game of dice is played in dream. Some characters like Eklavya, Aswasthama are fully changed. His use of myth is selective and is more implicit than explicit.

Apart from it, the mythological motif is treated by both the novelists Amitav Ghosh and Shashi Tharoor as a single myth in *The Circle of Reason* and that of *The Great Indian Novel*.

Novelists under the present study have used mythic prefigurations in different ways and for different purposes. R.K. Narayan uses myth as literary allusion, as illustration, and as a parallel in *The Man Eater of Malgudi*. Raja Rao's myth is as the collective consciousness and his fictional characters appear as incarnation as in *The Serpent and the Rope*. Salman Rushdie's myth is structural in principle in *Midnight's Children*. One can trace the maximum and multipurpose use of myth in the novel. His mythic characters are almost prefigurations. Amitav Ghosh's mythical character is Nachiketa as a protagonist in *The Circle of Reason*. In *The Great Indian Novel*, Shashi Tharoor's use of myth is structural in principle.

The analysis of the Indian English novels in the preceding chapters testifies that the Indian English creative writers have successfully projected structural variations of myth, which is well-foregrounded in the novel in the forms of Indian mythological, philosophical and narrative traditions. This is how our present writers connect themselves to thousands of years of old traditions by creating narratives in literature in the substantial way which contributes to the world of art and the world of metaphysical reality. Using myths from different Indian classics, the novelists have found the relevance and significance of these monumental myths in our time. Myth is a powerful weapon of these novelists which reveals their hidden potentialities. Indian English novelists have revived the mythic narrative traditions and evoked in their novels the collective consciousness of India's wisdom taken from the rich store of myths and legends. Mythic narratives, contributed to Indian English fiction, are the distinctive achievements of these novelists. Myth, in brief, is a metaphor, an image, an allusion, a symbol and a substitution for an object which has been skilfully and artistically used by these novelists. The book moderately claims that it would reveal some of the characteristics of the Indian English novels that have not been taken care of by scholarship in a meaningful way.

Select Bibliography

PRIMARY SOURCES

Ghosh, Amitav. *The Circle of Reason.* Hamish Hamilton, London, 1986.

———, *The Shadow Lines* (1988). New Delhi: Ravi Dayal Publishers, 1988.

———, *The Antique Land* (1992). New Delhi: Ravi Dayal Publishers, 1992.

———, *The Calcutta Chromosome* (1996). New Delhi: Ravi Dayal Publishers, 1998.

———, *The Glass Palace* (2000). New Delhi: Ravi Dayal Publishers, 2000.

Narayan, R.K. *Swami and Friends* (1935). Mysore: Indian Thought Publications, 1971.

———, *The Bachelor of Arts* (1936). Mysore: Indian Thought Publications, 1972.

———, *The Dark Room* (1938). Mysore: Indian Thought Publications, 1972.

———, *The English Teacher* (1945). Mysore: Indian Thought Publications, 1996.

———, *Mr. Sampath* (1949). Mysore: Indian Thought Publications, 1956.

———, *The Financial Expert* (1952). Mysore: Indian Thought Publications, 1984.

————, *The Man Eater of Malgudi* (1961). Mysore: Indian Thought Publication, 1994.

————, *Gods, Demons and Others* (1964). Mysore: Indian Thought Publication, 1973.

————, *My Days* (1975). London: Chatts and Windis, 1975.

————, *The Painter of Signs* (1976). Mysore: Indian Thought Publications, 1993.

————, *A Tiger for Malguddi*. Mysore: Indian Thought Publications, 1983.

————, *A Writer's Nightmare*. New Delhi: Penguin, 1987.

————, *The Ramayan*. New Delhi: Vision Book Pvt. Ltd. 1987.

Rao, Raja. *Kanthapura* (1938). New Delhi: Orient Paperbacks, 1971.

————, *The Serpent and the Rope* (1960). New Delhi: Orient Paperbacks, 1968.

————, *The Cat and Shakespeare* (1965). New Delhi: Hindi Pocket Books, 1971.

————, *Comrade Kirillov* (1976). New Delhi: Orient Paperback, 1976.

Rushide, Salman. *Grimus* (1975). London: Granada Publishing, 1982.

————, *Midnight's Children* (1981). London: Picador, 1981.

————, *Shame* (1983). New Delhi: Rupa & Co., 1983.

————, *The Ground Beneath Her Feet* (2000). London: Vintage, 2002.

Singh, Sunny. *Nani's Book of Suicides* (2002). New Delhi: Harper Collins Publishers India, 2002.

Tharoor, Shashi. *The Great India Novel* (1989). New Delhi: Penguin Books India, 1989.

SECONDARY SOURCES

1. Books:

Abrams, M.H. *A Glossary of Literary Terms*. Bangalore: Prism Books Pvt. Ltd., 1993.

Aggrawal, N.K. *Myths and Legends of India Retold*. Calcutta: Blackie and Sons, 1986.

Asnani, M. Shyam. *Critical Response to Indian English Fiction*. Delhi: Mittal Publications, 1985.

Agnihotri, G.N. *Indian Life and Problems in the Novels of Mulk Raj Anand, Raja Rao and R.K. Narayan*. Meerut: Shalabh Prakashan, 1993.

Beckson, Karl and Gan, Arthus. *A Reader's Guide to Literary Terms*. London: Thames and Hudson, 1972.

Biswal, K. Jayant. *A Critical study of the Novels of R.K. Narayan*. New Delhi: Nirmal Publishers, 1987.

Cassel's. *Encyclopaedia of Literature*. Vol. I, Ed. S.H. Steinberg. London: 1953.

Cassirer Ernst. *The Philosophy of Symbolic Forms*, Vol. 1, *Mythical Thought*, Tr. By Ralph Manheim, New Haven, Yale University Press, 1955.

Daiches, David. *Critical Approaches to Literature*. Bombay: Orient Longman, 1973.

Dewari, D.S. *The Use of Myth in R.K. Narayan's Novels*. New Delhi: Prestige Books, 2001.

Dimmit, Cornelia and J.A.B. Van Buitenen (ed. & tr.). *Classical Hindu Mythology: A Reader in Sanskrit Puranas*. Bombay: Rupa & Co., 1983.

Drew, Elizabeth and T.S. Eliot. *The Design of His Poetry*. Delhi: Doaba House, 1970.

Eliot, T.S. *Four Quartets*. Delhi: Oxford University Press, 1974.

Eliade, Mircea. *The Myth of the Eternal Return*. tr. from the

French by William R. Trask. London: Routledge & Kegan Paul Ltd., 1955.

Frye, Northrop. *Fables of Identity*. New York, 1963.

Gould, Eric. *Mythic Intentions in Modern Literature*. Princeton: Princeton University Press, 1981.

Hariprasanna, A. *The World of Malgudi: A Study of R.K. Narayan's Novels*. New Delhi: Prestige Books, 1994.

Hemenway, Stephan. *Raja Rao's Kanthaprna and The Serpent and the Rope*. Culcutta: A Writer's Workshop Publication, 1975.

Hutcheon Linda. *A Poetics of Postmodernism*. New York and London: Routledge, 1988.

Iyengar, K.R. Srinivas. *Indian Writing in English*. New Delhi: Sterling Publishers Private Limited, 1982.

Johnson, M. Harry. *Sociology: A Systematic Introduction*. New Delhi: Allied Publishers, 1980.

———, *Kathopanishad*. Gorakhpur: Geeta Press, Govind Bhavan.

Kirpal, Viney (ed.). *The New Indian Novel in English*. New Delhi: Allied Publishers, 1990.

Kirk, G.S. *Myth: Its Meaning and Function in Ancient and Other Cultures*. Cambridge. University of California Press, 1970.

Lal, D.K. *Myth and Mythical Concept in O'Neill's Plays*. New Delhi: Atlantic Publishers and Distributors, 1992.

Lal, P. *The Alien Insiders: Indian Writing in English*. Calcutta: Writer's Workshop, 1982.

Levi-Strauss, Claude. *Mythology*. Tr. By Rodney Needham, London: Merlin Press, 1964.

Masani, R.P. *Persian Mysticism: Being an Abridged Version of Farid-Ud-Din Attar's Matia-Ut-Tayr*. New Delhi: Award Publishing House, 1991.

Mathur, O.P. *Indian Political Novel*. Allahabad: Kitab Mahal, 1995.

McLeod, A.L. (Ed.). *R.K. Narayan Critical Perspectives*. New Delhi: Sterling Publishers Private Limited, 1994.

Mukherjee, Meenakshi. *The Twice Born Fiction*. Arnold Heinemann Publishers (India) Private Limited, 1974.

————, *Rushdie's Midnight Children A Book of Readings*. Penecraft International, 1999

Narayan, R.K. "God and the Atheist". In *A Writer's Nightmare*, New Delhi: Penguin, 1987.

Naipal, V.S. *India A Million Mutinies Now*, London: Minerva, 1990.

Naik, M.K. *The Ironic Vision: Study of the Fiction of R.K. Narayan*. New Delhi: Sterling Publications Pvt. Ltd., 1983.

————, *Raja Rao*. New York: Blackie & Son Publishers Pvt. Ltd., 1982.

Narasimhaiah, C.D. *The Swan & the Eagle*. New Delhi: Vision Books Pvt. Ltd., 1999.

Nehru, Jawaharlal. *The Discovery of India*. New Delhi: Oxford Univetsity Press, 1974.

————, *An Autobiography*. New Delhi: Oxford Press, 1982.

Organ, Troy Wilson. *The Hindu Quest for the Perfection of Man*. Athens: Ohio, Ohio University Press, 1970.

Otto, Rudolf. *The Idea of the Holy* (English tr.) London and New York, 1950.

Parameswaran, Uma. *The Perforated Sheet: Essays on Salman Rushide's Art*. New Delhi: Affiliated West Press Pvt. Ltd., 1988.

————, *A Study of the Representative Indo-English Novelists*. New Delhi: Vikas Publishing House, 1976.

Pallan, Rajesh K.: *Myths and Symbols in Raja Rao and R.K.Narayan* Jalandhar: A B S Publications,1994

Pallan, Rajesh K. *Indian English Fiction: A Select Study*. Jalandhar: Krishna Brothers, 1992.

Porter, Thomas E. *Myth and Modern American Drama*. Ludhiana: Kalyani Publishers, 1969.

Rai, V. *Use of Myth in the Poetry of Romantic Revival*, B.H.U., unpublished Ph.D. Thesis, 1959.

Raizada, Harish. *R.K. Narayan: A Critical Study of His Works*. New Delhi: Young Indian Publications, 1969.

Rao, A.S. *Myth and History in Contemporary Indian Novel in English*. New Delhi: Atlantic Publishers and Distributors, 2000.

Roy, Dulip Kumar. *The Bhagavadgita: A Revelation*. Delhi: Hindi Pocket Books, 1976.

Sankaran, Chitra. *The Myth Connection: The Use of Hindu Mythology in Some Novels of Raja Rao and R.K. Narayan*. Ahmedabad: Allied Publishers, 1993.

Sharan, Nagendra Nath. *A Critical Study of the Novels of R.K. Narayan*. New Delhi: Classical Publishing Company, 1993.

Sharma, K.K. (ed.). *Indo-Anglican Literature: A Collection of Critical Essays on Indian Creative Writers in English*. Ghaziabad: Vimal Prakashan, 1977.

Sharrad, Paul. *Raja Rao and Cultural Tradition*. New Delhi: Sterling Publishers Pvt. Ltd., 1987.

Srivastava, Narsingh. *The Mind and Art of Raja Rao*. Bareilly: Prakash Book Depot, 1980.

Sundaram, P.S. *R.K. Narayan as a Novelist*. Delhi: B.R. Publishing Corporation, 1988.

Thapar, Romilla. *Ancient Indian Social History*. New Delhi: Orient Longman, 1978.

Tiwari, Shubha, *Amitav Ghosh: Acticical Study*, New Delhi, Atlantic Publications, 2003.

Verma, R.M. *Some Aspects of Indo-English Fiction*. New Delhi: Jain Sons Publications, 1985.

Walsh, William. *R.K. Narayan: A Critical Appreciation*. New Delhi: Allied Publishers, 1983.

——————, *Indian Literature in English*. New York: Congman, 1990.

White, John J. *Mythologies in the Modern Novel*. Princeton: Princeton University Press, 1971.

——————, *Hindu Mythology: Vedic and Puranic*. Calcutta: Rupa & Co., 1973.

Williams, H.M. *Studies in Modern Indian Fiction in English*. Calcutta: Writers Workshop, 1973.

Zimmer, Heinrich. *Myths and Symbols in Indian Art and Civilization*. Ed. Joseph Campbell. Princeton: Princeton University Press, 1946.

——————, *Philosophies of India*. Ed. Joseph Campbell. Princeton: Princeton University Press, 1951.

2. Articles, Interviews and Journals:

Asnani, M. Shyam. "The Use of Myth in R.K. Narayan's Novels", *The Literary Endeavour*, Vol. III, nos. 3&4, April-June 1982.

Berry, Margaret. "R.K. Narayan: Lila and Literature", *The Journal of Indian Writing in English*, Vol. 4, no.2.

Benerjee, N.N. "Recent Indian Writing in English", *Contemporary Indian Literature*, Vol. 4 March 1964.

Chase, Richard. "Notes on the Study of Myth", *Twentieth Century Criticism: The Major Statements*. Ed. William J. Handy and Max Westbrook. New Delhi: Light and Life Publishers, 1970.

Chaturvedi, Nagesh. "Indian myths in Rushdie's Midnight's Children", *Language Forum*, Dec/June 1993.

Choudhury, M.K. "New Generation Indian English Novel", *Indian English Novel in the Nineties*. Ed. Sheobhushan Shukla. New Delhi: Sarup & Sons, 2002.

Frye, Northrop. "Anatomy of Criticism: Four Essays". Princeton: Princeton University Press, 1971.

__________, "Myth, Fiction and Displacement", *Twentieth Century Criticism: The Major Statements*. Ed. William J. Handy and max Wertbrook.

__________, "The Archetypes of Literature", *Twentieth Century Criticism: The Major Statements*.

Kripal, Viney. "Politics and Philosophy in the Great Indian Novel". *Littcrit*, 16. 1,2 (June/Dec., 1990).

Kumar, Prem Nand. "Shashi Tharoor's Karna". *Littcrit*, June/Dec, 1990.

Lal, P. "Mod Mahabharata". *Littcrit*, June /Dec 1990.

Lal, P. "Myth and the Indian Writers in English: A Note", *Aspects of Indian Writing in English*. Ed. M.K. Naik. Madras: Macmillan India, 1979.

Malinouski. "The Concept of Myth and Ritual in Literature", Ed. John Halloway, *Studies in Shakespeare's Major Tragedies*. London: Routledge & Kegan Paul, 1961.

Mathur, O.P. "Two Modern Versions of the Sita Myth: Narayan and Anand", *The Journal of Commonwealth Literature*, Vol. XXI, no. 1, 1986.

Max Muller, Friedrich. "Comparative Mythology", reprinted in *Selected Essays on Language, Mythology and Religion*. London, George Routledge, 1909.

Mukhopadhyaya, Aruna. "Collage of Myths: Amitav Ghosh's The Circle of Reason", Eds. R.S. Sharma & S.B. Shukla, *Studies in Contemporary Literature*. New Delhi: Sarup & Sons, 2000.

Narayan, R.K. "All India Radio Interview on September 8, 1961", *Writers Workshop Miscellany*, no. 8, 1961.

Narayan, Shyamala: "The structure of Amitav Ghosh's *The Circle of Reason*". *Littcrit*. June/Dec. 1988.

Paniker, K. Ayyappa. "Man and God in Indian American Fiction: A Study Based on Kanthapura, Arrow of God and Mookajji's Visions", *Commonwealth Literature Problems of Response*. Ed. C.D. Narasimhaiah. Madras: Macmillan, 1981.

Rao, Raja. "Books Which Have Influenced Me", *The Illustrated Weekly of India*. Bombay: February 10, 1963.

Raizada, Harish. "Point of View, Myth and Symbolism in Raja Rao's Novels", *Perspectives on Raja Rao*. Ed. K.K. Sharma. Ghaziabad: Vimal Prakashan, 1980.

Rushdie, Salman. "Reclaiming a city and a History". *Express Magazine* (The Indian Express, March 11, 1984).

Schorer, Mark. "The Necessity of Myth" in *Myth and Myth Making* ed. *A. Murray Boston: Beacon Press*, 1960.

Shklovsky Victor. "Arts as Technique", *Modern Criticism and Theory- A Reader*, ed. David Lodge, London and New York; Longman, 1988.

Singh, R.S. "A European Brahmin: Raja Rao", *Indian Writing in English*. New Delhi: Arnold Heinemann, 1977.

Srivastasva, Narsingh. "Love and Divorce in *The Serpent and the Rope*", *Quest*, no. 97, September and October, 1975.

Tharoor, Shashi. "Yoking Myth to History". *Littcrit*, June/Dec. 1990.

Index

A

Abrams, M.H.3
Agnihotri, 17,18
Antique Land, An 103
Asnani, Shyam M. 60,71

B

Bachelor of Arts, The 18

C

Calcutta Chromosome, The 103
Cassell 1
Cassirer, Ernst 4,5
Cat and Shakespeare, The 17,18,28
Chase, Richard 7,11
Chaturvedi, Nagesh 87,88
Circle of Reason, The 103, 104, 109, 115, 119, 120

D

Daiches, David, 6
Dark Room, The 19,55
Dewari, D.S. 12
Dhawan, R.K. 103
Drew, Elizabeth, 2, 9

E

Eliade, Mircea 2, 15,16
Eliot, T.S. 9,72
English Teacher, The 55, 56
Financial Expert, The 19, 58, 59

F

Frye, Northrop 3, 4, 7, 10, 11

G

Ghosh, Amitav 103
Glass Palace, The 104
Gods, Demons and others 54
Great Indian Novel, The 20, 22, 122, 123, 124, 125, 126, 138, 139
Grimus 20
Ground Beneath Her Feet, The 20,77,78

H

Hemenway, Stephan 40
Hutcheon, Linda 79

I

Iyengar, K.R. Srinivas 63

J

Jameson, Frederic 133
Johnson, Harry M.20
Jung, C.G. 4

K

Kanthapura 17,28,29
Kathopanishad, 105,112
Kirpal, Viney 124,136
Kothandaraman, Bala 104
Krishna, M. Sivaram 129
Kumar, Prem Nanda 131

L

Lal, D.K. 12
Lal, P.2, 136
Lawrence, D.H. 9
Levi-Strauss, Claude 5
Lukacs, George 83

M

Mahabharata, The 14, 15, 21, 26, 28, 30, 33, 50, 122, 123, 124, 127, 138, 139

Malinouski 2,3

Man Eater of Malgudi, The 18, 19, 60, 61, 62, 68, 71,72

Mani, D.S. 40

Mathur, O.P. 33, 78, 79

Max Muller, Friedrich, 4

Midnight's Children 20, 76, 79, 80, 81, 82, 83, 84, 85, 86, 88, 93, 94, 95, 96, 97, 98, 99, 101, 124

Mukherjee, Meenakshi 8, 14, 15, 17, 32, 66, 70

Mukhopadhyaya, Aruna 119

My Days 52

N

Naik, M.K. 28,32,61,63,68

Naipaul, V.S. 13

Nani's Book of Suicides 21,22

Narasimhaiah, C.D. 29, 30, 42, 48, 98, 138

Narayan, R.K. 12, 52, 53, 54, 58, 60, 63, 68, 71, 72

Narayan, Shyamala A 117, 119, 120

Nehru, Jawahar Lal 15, 125, 126

Niranjan, Shiv 27

O

Olinder, Britta 52

P

Painter of Signs, The 59

Pallan, Rajesh K. 6, 14, 71

Parameswaran, Uma 83

Parthsarthy, R. 29

Puranas 13, 14, 15, 27, 50, 53

R

Rai, V. 1

Raizada, Harish 35, 54

Ramaswamy, S.45

Ramayana, The 14,15, 17, 26, 29, 42, 50, 53, 55

Rao, A.S. 76, 98

Rao, K.R. 100

Rao, Raja 26, 27, 28, 29, 30, 32, 33, 49

Rushdie, Salman 78, 82

S

Sampath, Mr. 56,57

Sankaran, Chitra 14,30,58

Schorer, Mark, 1

Serpent and the Rope, The 17, 18, 26, 29, 32, 33, 34, 35, 36, 37, 38, 39, 40, 41, 42, 43, 44, 45, 46, 47, 48,49, 50

Shadowlines, The 103

Shame 20,77

Sharan, Nagendra Nath, 34,

Shklovsky, Victor 137

Singh, R.S. 43

Srivastava, Narsingh 45

Sundaram, P.S. 60, 65

Swami and Friends 18, 54

T

Thapar, Romilla 3

Tharoor, Shashi 123,124

Tiger for Malgudi, A 60

Tiwari, Shubha 120

W

Waiting for Mahatma 59

Walsh, William 67,78

White, John J. 88,108

Writer's Nightmare, A 72

Z

Zimmer, Heirich 35,59